Congressional Budgeting

A Representational Perspective

Patrick Fisher

University Press of America,® Inc.
Lanham · Boulder · New York · Toronto · Oxford

352.48
F53c

To my parents,
Fred and Claudia Fisher

Contents

List of Tables and Figures

Tables

Figures

Preface

Putting together the federal budget in undoubtably an enormous task. Given the size and scope of the American government, it can be said that congressional budgeting is an almost futile undertaking. Indeed, Congress faces a formidable endeavor when trying to put together a budget that is roughly in balance. Yet, this has not always been the case. For most of American history, Congress was regularly able to produce balanced budgets. The budgetary dynamics that Congress faces today, however, are considerably different than the dynamics of a century ago or even forty years ago.

Congress as an institution is as unpopular today as it ever has been. Large deficits unquestionably play a roll in the public's disapproval of Congress. Deficits are important symbolically because they make Congress look inept. And most members of Congress acknowledge the problem. Yet, Congress is unable to fix the problem. To a significant degree, this is because Congress is following the dictates of public opinion. The conflicting desires of the American public create enormous difficulties for Congress when it produces the nation's budget.

This book will analyze the problems inherent in the congressional budget process and will undertake to understand why Congress makes the budgetary decisions it does. If Congress produces such inadequate budgets, can't Congress simply changes the way it budgets? In some ways it seems simple. If it is clear that the budget is not going to be balanced, why not simply change budget priories?

Congress is designed for budgeting in the 19th Century, not for the 21st Century. Structurally, Congress is a budgeting disaster. The budget process is extremely decentralized and parochial. In their desire to limit the "tyranny of the majority," the framers of the Constitution designed a legislature that would be constrained and deliberate. Yet, while the institutional structure of Congress (i.e. bicameralism and the committee system) and American government in general (i.e. separation of powers) make the budget process more difficult, it does not make producing a sensible budget impossible.

Rather, it is the representational nature of Congress that makes budgeting such a flawed process. Budgeting requires Congress to compromise parochial interests for the well being of the entire nation. The budget process necessitates that members of Congress compromise to make macro-level budget decisions. This is something that Congress has found it extremely difficult to do. The parochial nature of congressional budgeting is the key to understanding the predicament Congress confronts when budgeting.

Chapter 1

Introduction

The Contradictions of Congressional Budgeting

The congressional budget process is much maligned. Seemingly anyone who comments on the congressional budget process deems it unsatisfactory. The arduous process itself would be less problematic if it were not for the consistency in which the process has tended to lead to large budget deficits over the past three decades. This work examines the congressional budget process in an attempt to establish the demands upon Congress which lead it to favor budgets where expenditures consistently outpace revenues.

Congress's difficulty in budgeting is in part institutional and in part political. This book presents an analysis of possible structural and representational explanations for the problems endemic to congressional budgeting. Though the institutional dynamics of the budget process make budgeting more problematic, it is the contention of this work that it is primarily due to political reasons that Congress finds it so difficult to produce balanced budgets. Specifically, the nature of congressional representation makes budgeting an extremely formidable task for Congress. A central question that will be examined in this work is what precisely about political representation in the United States affects the budget process adversely?

The difficulties Congress has in budgeting are a direct result of the nature of a representative democracy. When it comes to congressional budgeting, democratic representation is a paradox because the American public wants contradictory actions from its representatives in Congress. The public wants lower taxes, does not want its government services cut, and wants a balanced budget to boot. If the role of a member of Congress is to represent the wishes of his or her constituents, something has got to give. For the most part this has been balancing the budget.

Congress and Deficits

Does the congressional budget process work? There are of course many potential ways to measure "success," but for the purposes of this work we will look at the bottom line–does the process allow Congress to produce budgets that over the long haul will be reasonably in balance? And the answer to that question is a resounding NO! As a result, the deficit "has become the most prominent symbol in American politics."[1]

A structural deficit is one that is endemic to the system while a cyclical deficit is one that is caused by a temporary downturn in the economy. With the exception of 1998-2001, the U.S. government has experienced deficits every year since 1969 (see Table 1.1). It can thus be argued that the deficit in this country has become a structural deficit. Chronic deficit spending has been widely regarded as the most conspicuous failure of the American budget process. In 1970, the total federal debt was $283 billion, or 28 percent of the Gross National Product (GNP). By 1994, the debt topped the $3 trillion mark, or 50 percent of the GNP.

Most economists argue that balancing the budget unquestionably needs to be combined with flexibility in order to respond to changing needs or to downturns in the economy.[2] Yet most economists also hold that chronic deficits are problematic. Deficits have severe effects on the budget process and the domestic economy. The Ricardian Equivalence Theorem, for example, argues that an increase in government debt is effectively equivalent to a future increase in tax liabilities; therefore, an increase in the federal debt is not judged to be an addition to private wealth.[3] Thus, not only will efforts to reduce the deficit impinge on other spending, but the long-term cost of paying for the accumulated deficits will soak up a major portion of available resources in the future. As a result, a potential result of the deficit spending of the last three decades is that there will be little opportunity to expand government programs in the future, even when there is a broad consensus to do so.[4] Large chronic budget deficits, therefore, have the potential to tie the hands of future

Table 1.1
The Federal Deficit and the National Debt
(In billions of $)

Year	Federal Deficit (-) or Surplus (+)	Total Public Debt	Debt as % of GNP
1970	-12	283	28.1
1975	-69	395	25.4
1980	-61	710	26.1
1985	-212	1,500	36.2
1990	-221	2,411	42.0
1991	-269	2,688	45.3
1992	-290	3,000	48.2
1993	-255	3,249	49.5
1994	-203	3,433	49.4
1995	-164	3,605	49.2
1996	-108	3,735	49.9
1997	-22	3,773	47.3
1998	+69	3,722	44.3
1999	+124	3,633	39.9
2000	+236	3,410	35.1
2001	+127	3,320	33.1
2002	-158	3,540	34.3
2003	-375	3,914	36.1

Source: Congressional Budget Office

policy makers for years to come.

The fact that our government is paying such enormous sums just on the interest of our nation debt leads us to the question of the effects of the debt on future generations. Budgeting should be concerned with its generational effects. We should concern ourselves with the extent to which current actions will improve or harm the conditions that older, younger, and future generations must confront.

For conservatives, deficits mean higher tax rates for future generations to pay for interest on the national debt; for liberals, future payments on interest on the national debt due to the deficits of the past three decades are a lost opportunity to pay for government programs in areas such as education and health care. Thus, in budget preparation, the projection of budget deficits should be an overriding issue that cannot be ignored since deficits can be seen as people today engaging services that will be paid for by their children and grandchildren.

Since the 1970s, most scholars who have studied the federal budget process have been extremely pessimistic regarding the ability of the federal government to produce balance budgets. It has been widely held that large deficits were probably inevitable in the foreseeable future.[5] Furthermore, as the Baby Boom generation approaches retirement age, long term projections of budget deficits seemed to indicate that matters would only get worse.

Throughout the history of the United States, however, the concept of balanced budgets and steady reduction in the real debt has had a stable majority constituency.[6] The emergence of large and rapidly increasing federal budget deficits after 1970, following 180 years of (approximately) balanced budgets except periods of war or recession, constitutes an historical abnormality. Large deficits not related to war or depression are a very recent development in American history.[7] So why do large federal budget deficits now seem almost inevitable? Possible explanations include: excessive spending, insufficient taxing, institutional obstacles, public opinion, and the nature of congressional representation.

Excessive Spending

Adam Smith attributes the public debt to three influences: the desire of government officials to spend, the unpopularity of raising taxes, and the willingness of capitalists to lend.[8] Thus, he sees government debt as an accompaniment of a capitalistic society. The result is that if political leaders are expected to continue providing a constant volume of services, make increased interest payments, and keep taxes down, they will have to respond with even greater deficits. Most industrialized democracies have tended to run budget deficits in the post-war period because they have found it easy to spend and difficult to tax. Even though governments have the power to tax, summoning the will to tax is often a stumbling block preventing more closely balanced budgets. Governments historically have encountered difficulty in mustering the will to levy new or increased taxes, and this tendency appears to have proliferated since the 1970s.[9] At the same time it is easy and politically desirable for governments to spend money. Thus, there are biases in the political and economic systems which drive budgetary outcomes toward deficits.

The modern conventional justification for public debt emerged with John Maynard Keynes.[10] Government, he believed, must take an active role in promoting full employment through both fiscal and monetary policy. To Keynes, classical economics failed to recognize that the market cannot by itself adequately maintain consumption demands and coordinate investment decisions. Keynesian economics, however, has come under increasing attack as deficits have skyrocketed. Critics argue that Keynesians severely neglected politics and the political process by ignoring public choice implications. Policy advocacy, according to this argument, must always be placed squarely in a political setting and must be aware of the incentive structure that faces persons in their varying public choosing roles as voters, as party leaders, as elected politicians, as bureaucrats. Keynesian economics, fails to do this, critics argue, encouraging deficits.[11]

The postwar transformation of federal budgeting from a control process to one oriented toward spending growth has upset the relationship between available resources and demands on the budget. Claims on the budget became stronger when budgeting was an expansionary process, and it has not been easy for Congress to reverse course as the climate has become more constrained. Budgeting for growth (1950s-1960s) differs from budgeting for stabilization or cutback (1970s-1990s). The expectation of growth makes it easier to please greater numbers of actors because government can afford to give people what they want.[12] This transformed budgetary environment became a long-term threat to Congress' power of the purse because Congress had become unwilling, for political reasons, to control spending.[13] Congress saw its ability to manage spending decline as the costs of government have increased.[14] Incentives to spend are greater than the incentives to control spending. In particular, those who advocate spending often have greater success in political mobilization relative to mobilization by those who finance the spending.[15]

A particular type of spending that is widely seen as being

difficult to control is entitlement spending. The rapid growth of entitlements has given them a bad name in some quarters because they are held to blame for deficits. Some of the most expensive programs in the federal budget are entitlements such as Social Security and Medicare; they are also politically the most hazardous to alter and it is widely perceived that legislators would rather look elsewhere for ways to cut spending.

During the 1960s and 1970s, budgeting became further complicated by what became known as "backdoor" spending, meaning spending authority provided outside of the normal appropriations process. The effect of backdoor spending was that virtually all committees in Congress came to play important roles in financial decisions, with no mechanism to coordinate their diverse activities. Various forms of backdoor spending (contract authority, borrowing authority, and entitlements) have been employed by authorizing committees to circumvent the appropriations committees and to create spending obligations that must be met. The result has been the growth of open-ended spending commitments, whose impact on the budget has risen dramatically since the 1960s.[16]

In terms of controlling spending, the 1974 Budget Act has been blamed for magnifying the problems of the budget process. Certainly, the 1974 Budget Act failed to be the panacea that supporters had hoped it might be. In fact, many of the act's provisions have had a negative impact on attempts to balance the budget. Some go as far as to suggest that the 1974 Budget Act is largely responsible for the gigantic deficits of the 1980s because it has failed to control spending. By expanding Congress's flexibility in making decisions on spending, the act may have encouraged higher spending. Among those provisions of the act that have encouraged higher spending include the preferred status it gives entitlements, the fact that it encourages greater advocacy by congressional committees, and the adoption of generous budget resolutions that serve as floors rather than ceilings on expenditures.[17]

Insufficient Taxing

The tax side of the budget should be considered equal to the spending side of the budget in its political and economic importance. As mentioned above, many place the blame for skyrocketing deficits on the inability of Congress to limit spending. But one can just as easily argue that it is the inability of Congress to tax enough that makes it so difficult for the federal government to balance the budget. In particular, the declining progressivity of the federal income tax may be making it more difficult for the federal government to get the required revenue to balance the budget. Since the end of World War II, the federal tax system has gradually become less progressive, as the corporate income tax has declined substantially while payroll taxes have increased substantially. It may be that it is the obstacles the American political system places on raising revenues that makes Congress look so inadequate at budgeting. The congressional system has a bias against active consideration of certain issues, and taxes can be considered one of these issues.[18]

Americans tend to dislike government spending in the abstract, but to welcome it for the specific programs. Members of Congress face a dilemma in that voters would like more benefits for the same or lower taxes. The need for periodic tax increases, however, is an important link between the taxpayers and the government, keeping government expenditures in line with the desires of the taxpayers.[19] Taxes may not be popular, but there is no way for the government to function without them.

Increasing taxes, even if it is concentrated mainly on upper incomes, is a hard political sell even if the goal is to reduce the deficit.[20] Deficit reduction requires one to think in terms of the long run, which is difficult for voters as well as policy makers to do. Tax increases, however, are evident immediately, and therefore much more of a factor at the ballot box. Distributing the hardships of budget cuts and tax increases is much more problematic than distributing the benefits of surplus.[21]

Deficits can thus been seen to be a result of the inability of Congress to either constrain spending enough or to tax sufficiently. But why is Congress unable to tax adequately or to control spending sufficiently to produce balanced budgets?

Institutional Obstacles

To some, it is the weakness of the procedures Congress has adopted, not a weakness of will, that makes government unable to live within its means.[22] Congress is not designed to focus on long-term budgeting. Deficit-cutting is not pleasant. Taxes have to go up or spending needs to be cut. Voters do not like either option. Since the effects of deficits on living standards might not be apparent for two decades or more, why would today's elected officials, whose incentives revolve around electoral needs, want to anger today's voters? Short-term politics discourages thinking about long-term budget consequences.[23]

Outside of Congress, separation of powers is a potential institutional obstacle in the creation of a balanced budget. The power of the purse is one of the central powers of Congress, and was designed as such by the Founding Fathers. Due to the fear of "taxation without representation," there was an early recognition that financial issues would be primarily congressional concerns. Throughout the nineteenth century Congress considered itself to be the dominate branch of government, and it had relatively little contact with the White House on budgetary matters. As government grew in size and scope, however, Congress found itself forced to give up its powers over the purse gradually to the president. Even with an increasingly centralized budget process, however, Congress has had more and more difficulty limiting expenditures to revenues. In order to cut the deficit, therefore, it makes sense to delegate budgetary authority to the president. This allows Congress to duck blame for making tough political decisions. Presidential policy thus is also held to blame for large deficits.[24] Furthermore, it is possible that the prevalence of divided government has made it more difficult to balance the budget because the president and Congress could not agree on priorities.

Another factor leading to deficits may be the increased partisanship within Congress itself. Extreme partisanship may work against producing a balanced budget. The congressional budget process became increasingly polarized among partisan lines during the 1980s and 1990s. Congressional districts represented by Democratic members of Congress are significantly different demographically and politically from those districts represented by Republicans. This dynamic has the potential to dramatically influence the manner in which Congress is able to make the compromises necessary to produce a balanced budget.[25] Also, divided government may work to reinforce the differences in budgetary priorities among the parties. Political parties are needed to provide a sense of collective responsibility for the consequences of what is in the budget, but it is possible that extreme partisanship could lead to stalemate and thus make it more difficult to balance the budget.

Public Opinion

Rather than blaming institutional obstacles, it is possible to attribute the prevalence of budget deficits on the fact that the American public seemingly wants contradictory budgetary actions from its representatives. The problems that federal officials face when budgeting are in part a result of the inconsistencies of what the public says it wanted.[26] Although the public clearly disapproves of deficits, it also tends to object to doing anything conclusive and drastic about them–a state of opinion reflected in the actions of the federal government. Polls showed that while the federal government was producing large deficits in the 1980s and early 1990s most respondents voiced a concern about the deficit but at the same time were reluctant to pay higher taxes and were opposed to suggested program cuts.[27] The large deficits of the 1980s and early 1990s may be said to be reasonably in accord with the preferences of the mass public.[28] Thus, deficits were in part the result of the fact the members of Congress and the White House listened to their constituents.[29]

The public's lack of concern toward the nation running in the red can be seen in their political responses. Citizens tend to worry more about the deficit when the economy is bad.[30] Thus, during the Reagan administration, the public's fear of the deficit declined as the economy improved. Reagan is the classic example of the fact that voters do not punish politicians for large deficits. In an April, 1984 poll, voters were asked, "Regardless of your own political views, what would you give as the best reason for voting against President Reagan?" The deficit ranked ninth with four percent, far behind foreign policy (21 percent) and fairness (18 percent).[31] Thus, even though deficits skyrocketed during his administration, it was not a factor in the 1984 elections as Reagan won in a landslide.

The Nature of Congressional Representation

When producing the budget, members of Congress take care of parochial interests as well as promoting national public interests. Legislators are therefore caught between conflicting demands. Since members must appease the desires of their constituency to win reelection, national budget interests may often be forced to take a back seat to local budget interests. If one thinks of government as deriving its powers for abstract considerations such as "what is best for the people," then a large national debt does not makes sense. But if one begins to think of human nature as the common denominator of both the governed and the governors, it is logical. One party wants a product (winning re-election), the other the money (government services). In swapping, each serves the self-interest of the other. Members of Congress, therefore, can be regarded as being exempt from repaying the debts they create.[32]

In a representative democracy such as the United States, one would expect a representative to be significantly influenced by his or her constituency.[33] Constituency interests undeniably play an important role in congressional decision-making. Since members of Congress would like to be reelected, constituency pressures impose meaningful constraints on voting behavior.[34] Representatives who desire to win reelection can be expected to act in concurrence with the preferences of their constituents.[35] Members of Congress will thus be attentive to the people that they are elected to represent, and studies have found strong evidence of dyadic representation on roll call voting.[36] Due to the nature of congressional representation, members of Congress have parochial interests when it comes to budgeting. The United States is a vast and diverse nation and taxing and spending issues inevitably affect constituencies differently.

Congress was created in order to provide a mechanism through which the people's preferences could be translated into public policy. Congress, however, is not a neutral institution making laws which benefit all citizens of the United States equally. The decisions arrived at by Congress have varying consequences for citizens, depending on the demographics of their constituents. Since individual districts tend to be relatively homogeneous, but heterogeneous as a whole (that is, they vary among each other), if we expect members of Congress to be responsive to the wishes of their constituents, it follows that members of Congress will represent their constituents differently, depending upon the characteristics of their district.[37] The heterogeneity of electorates, in fact, has been found to be an important factor in determining roll call votes.[38] The demographic characteristics of constituencies substantially affect the explanation of roll call votes.[39] Thus, citizen preferences may be expected to vary according to their demographic characteristics, which in turn influences the political behavior of their representatives in Congress.

To measure constituency influence, throughout this book (in

chapters 3, 4, 5, and 7) constituency demographics are tested as possible predictors of the political behavior of the district's representative on budgetary issues. Predictors chosen in this endeavor include the district's per capita income, the percentage of the district that has attended college, the percentage of the population that is white, and the percentage of the population that lives in rural areas. These predictors are chosen with the belief that these variables represent a diverse sample of constituency demographics, each measuring a separate aspect of the constituency–wealth, education, race, and urbanism.

There are a number of reasons we might expect these predictors to shape budget decisions. The higher a district's per capita income, the more reluctant a representative may be to support tax increases, since that representative's constituents would probably pay a disproportionate amount of the increased revenues. At the same time, the constituents of poorer districts may make it more difficult for their representative to support balanced budget policies because these districts have potentially the most to lose by cutting federal spending. In other words, the fact that the wealthy would have the most to lose with increased taxes and the poor the most to lose with decreased spending may put pressure on representatives with constituencies that have high and low per capita income levels to be hostile to particular types of balanced budget legislation. The percentage of college educated people in a district may be expected to influence a representative's budgetary decisions in a similar manner–it may be that the higher the education levels in a district, the more likely the constituency is to support conservative economic measures because income levels tend to be strongly related to education levels. On the other hand, higher education levels may make districts more likely to support more liberal economic measures because college educated people may have more realistic expectations for the budget and realize that taxes may have to be raised if services are to be maintained or if the deficit is to be reduced.

In terms of racial demographics, it may be expected that districts with a higher proportion of minorities would be expected to support more liberal budgetary actions by their representative because minorities in the United States tend to be more supportive of liberal candidates. Such a conclusion would also be consistent with previous findings.[40] Finally, the higher the percentage of people living in rural areas may lead to an increase in the district's inclination toward supporting a representative who advocates conservative budgetary policies since rural areas may see less benefit to increased social programs, but it may make the district more likely to elect a representative who supports liberal budgetary policies because rural areas tend to have lower levels of income.

To measure a district's political leanings, presidential vote totals in 1992 (a rough, tough imperfect, indicator of the district's political leanings) are analyzed in chapters 3, 4, 5, and 7 as a possible predictor of congressional budgetary actions. It would be expected, for example, that those districts that gave Clinton a higher percentage of the vote would more likely elect representatives who would support Clinton budgetary policies. Districts that gave Ross Perot a higher percentage of the 1992 presidential vote, on the other hand, may be the home of representatives who tended to dislike Clinton proposals because they did not cut spending enough, a criticism that Perot made after Clinton proposed his 1993 budget blueprint. It is possible, however, that those coming from a district with a higher Perot vote may have tended to support Clinton budgetary policy because they put a premium on deficit reduction–as a candidate Perot advocated both massive spending cuts and tax increases to reduce the deficit.

Potential factors representing characteristics of individual members are also chosen in subsequent chapters as possible determinants of budgetary action. The percentage of the vote that the representative received in their last general election is chosen as a variable to determine if previous electoral success meant that one would be more likely to support a potentially unpopular budget measures.[41] The number of years the representative served in the House or Senate is another variable analyzed. Since those with more seniority tend to come from politically "safer" districts and have more of a stake in appeasing the political leadership of the party, it may be that those with more years in their respective bodies are more likely to follow the lead of their party.[42] On the other hand, electoral safety may make a legislator more likely to be a "maverick" who supports deficit reduction measures that might not be popular with the party leadership. A legislator's party unity score–the percentage of the time the representative voted for a majority of their party against a majority of the other party–is analyzed as a variable with the belief that those who tend to support their party more often in general were also the most likely to support the position of their party on budgetary matters. Similarly, the presidential support scores of members of Congress is chosen as a variable in order to determine the influence of the White House on congressional budget decisions. Finally, to measure the importance of a representative's ideology, a member's floor vote history (as measured by the *National Journal* for the 103rd Congress) is analyzed to study the degree by which budgetary votes are consistent with other votes the member made.

The Rise and Fall of the Federal Budget Surplus

For a few years at the turn of the twentieth century, the dynamics of the federal budget process radically changed. After the federal budget deficit peaked at $290 billion in 1992, the nation's budgetary picture improved dramatically for the rest of the decade. In a development that would have been thought impossible in the early 1990s, there were actually budget surpluses from 1998-2001, the first years since 1969 that the federal government had not run in the red. In 2000, Clinton's last year as president, the federal government had a surplus of a staggering $236 billion, the eighth consecutive year with a declining deficit or increased surplus, a postwar record. As one budget scholar claims, "liquidating the deficit ranks as one of the supreme budgetary accomplishments in American history."[43] Symbolically, the fact that the federal government was able to produce surpluses was important because it suggests that federal budget deficits are not necessarily endemic to the system.

In order to reduce a budget deficit, policy makers must either raise taxes, cut spending, or hope that economic growth leads to increased revenues. The elimination of budget deficits in the late 1990s were due in part to all three of these techniques–income taxes were raised significantly in 1993, some spending was cut, and the economy performed remarkably well. Both Republicans and Democrats can therefore legitimately claim some credit for the reduction of the federal budget deficit. Republicans initiated numerous spending cuts after winning control of Congress in 1994 while Democrats were responsible for the increased revenues made possible by the passage of the 1993 Budget Reconciliation Bill which increased the income tax rates on the wealthiest Americans.

Figure 1.1
Deficits and Surpluses as a Share of the GDP

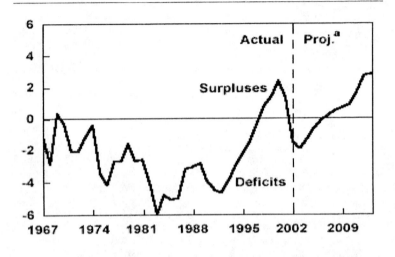

a = These projections incorporate the assumption that discretionary budget authority totals $751 billion for 2003 and grows with inflation thereafter.
Source: Congressional Budget Office

It has been suggested that the federal government was able to produce budget surpluses by cutting across the board or where it was politically easy to do so.[44] Regardless of the utility of the spending cuts, however, the spending reductions that took place throughout the 1990s did not account for most of the reduction of the federal budget deficit. While the spending reductions of both the 1990 Budget Act and 1993 Budget Reconciliation Bill have certainly contributed to the reduction of the deficit, overall spending outlays by the federal government continued to increase greater than the rate of inflation. The primary reason for the elimination of the budget deficit was the ability of the federal government to dramatically increase revenues. One reason for the increased revenues was strong economic growth. The strength of the economy, however, does not on its own account for the budget's turnaround.[45] After it became law, the 1993 Budget Reconciliation Bill, which raised the top income tax bracket from 31 percent to 36 and 39.6 percent, was extraordinarily successful at bringing in more revenue. The reason for the significant increase in revenues, therefore, was the combination of the progressive nature of the tax increases coupled with a very strong economy.[46]

The exact opposite scenario has occurred during the George W. Bush administration (see Figure 1.1). While the Clinton administration consistently underestimated the revenues that the federal treasury would bring in, the Bush administration has consistently overestimated future revenues. After George W. Bush was elected president he used the record surpluses at the time he was inaugurated to justify tax cuts, arguing the government had the money to spare. Within two years of his inauguration, however, the federal government was once again running in the red, as the tax cuts were enacted at the same time the economy stagnated, resulting in a tremendous decline in revenues.

The fact that a surplus of more than $200 billion in 2000 became a deficit of greater than $300 billion by 2003 demonstrates the inherent pull of the federal budget process towards deficits. The surpluses from 1998-2001 were unquestionably the exception rather than the rule. And with deficits now projected for the rest of the decade, we are forced once again to ask ourselves: what exactly about the budget process makes it so difficult for Congress to produce balanced budgets?

The Organization of the Book

Chapter 2 describes the factors that play a role in the spending and taxing decisions Congress makes. Chapters 3-5 examine institutional obstacles to the congressional budget process. Chapter 3 studies institutional dynamics of the congressional budget process that make budgeting problematic. Chapter 4 considers the role of the president in the budget process and identifies the problems that the constitutionally mandated separation of powers creates for the budget process, with a particular emphasis on Congress's inability to defend its budgetary powers from encroachment from the president. Chapter 5 analyzes the role that the political parties play in the budget process.

Chapters 6-7 examine representational obstacles to the congressional budget process. Chapter 6 will look at the inconsistencies of public opinion on budgetary matters. Finally, in Chapter 7, the book concludes with an examination of how the nature of congressional representation, especially the role of the constituency, affects how members of Congress make budget decisions. The conflicting desires of the American public, it is argued, create enormous difficulties for Congress when it produces the nation's budget.

A multitude of factors make budgeting difficult for Congress and throughout this work we will analyze these problems. The overriding theme, however, is that while structural explanations may be part of the problem, the main obstacle Congress faces in budgeting is a result of the nature of congressional representation. Though structural factors may complicate efforts to cope with the problem, it must be remembered that most of the institutional structures in place today existed when deficits were not a chronic problem. Some representational dynamics, however, changed as chronic deficits began to plague the budget process. It is the representational impediments to the budget process that are instrumental in understanding the problems facing congressional budgeting today.

Endnotes

1. Donald F. Kettl, *Deficit Politics* (New York: Longman, 2003), p. 21.

2. Irene Rubin, *Balancing the Federal Budget* (New York: Chatham House, 2003), p. 23-24.

3. R.J. Barro, "Are Government Bonds Net Wealth?" *Journal of Political Economy* 82 (1974): 1095-1117.

4. John Cranford, *Budgeting for America*, 2nd ed. (Washington, D.C.: CQ Press, 1989), p. 14.

5. Dennis Ippolito, *Congressional Spending* (Ithaca: Cornell University Press, 1981); John Cranford, *Budgeting for America*, 2nd ed. (Washington: CQ Press, 1989); Joseph White and Aaron Wildavsky *The Deficit and the Public Interest* (Berkeley: University of California Press, 1989); Allen Schick, *The Capacity to Budget* (Washington: Urban Institute,1990); Daniel Franklin, *Making Ends Meet* (Washington: CQ Press, 1993); Aaron Wildavsky and Naomi Caiden, *The Politics of the Budgetary Process*, 4th ed. (New York: Longman, 2001).

6. Gary Anderson, "The U.S. Federal Deficit and National Debt: A Political and Economic History," *Deficits*, James Buchanan, Charles Rowley, and Robert Tollison eds., pp. 9-35 (New York: Basil Blackwell Ltd., 1987).

7. Dennis Ippolito, *Why Budgets Matter: Budget Policy and American Politics* (University Park: Pennsylvania State University Press, 2003).

8. Adam Smith, *An Inquiry into the Nature and Causes of the Wealth of Nations* (New Rochelle, NY: Arlington House, 1961).

9. B. Guy Peters , *The Politics of Taxation* (Cambridge, MA: Blackwell., 1991).

10. John Maynard Keynes, *The General Theory of Employment, Interest, and Money* (New York: Harcourt Brace Jovanovich,1937).

11. James Buchanan, "Budgetary Bias in Post-Keynesian Politics," *Deficits*, James Buchanan, Charley Rowley and Robert Tollison editors, pp. 56-78 (New York: Basil Blackwell Ltd, 1987).

12. Schick (1990).

13. Ippolito (1981).

14. Cranford (1989).

15. Ron T. Meyers, *Strategic Budgeting* (Ann Arbor: University of Michigan Press. 1994).

16. Robert Lee and Ronald Johnson, *Public Budgeting Systems*, 5th edition (Gaithersburg, MD: Aspen Publishers, 1994).

17. Louis Fisher, "Ten Years After the Budget Act: Still Searching for Controls," *Public Budgeting* 5 (1985): 3-28.

18. Allen Schick, *Congress and Money* (Washington: AEI, 1980).

19. Sven Steinmo, *Taxation and Democracy* (New Haven: Yale University Press, 1993).

20. Patrick Fisher, "Political Explanations for the Difficulties in Congressional Budgeting," *The Social Science Journal* 36 (1999): 149-161.

21. Franklin (1993), p. 50.

22. Cranford (1989).

23. Lawrence Haas, *Running on Empty* (Homewood, IL: Business One Irvin, 1990).

24. Ivan W. Morgan, *Deficit Government* (Chicago: Ivan R. Dee, 1995).

25. Patrick Fisher, "The Prominence of Partisanship in the Congressional Budget Process," *Party Politics* 5 (1999): 225-236.

26. Allen Schick, "The Majority Rules," *The Brookings Review* 14 (1996): 42-55.

27. Ibid.

28. White and Wildavsky (1989).

29. Fisher, "Political Explanations for the Difficulties in Congressional Budgeting" (1999).

30. White and Wildavsky (1989).

31. Ibid., pp. 427-28.

32. Cole S. Brembeck, *Congress, Human Nature, and the Federal Debt* (New York: Praeger, 1991).

33. Benjamin I. Page, Robert Y. Shapiro, Paul W. Gronke and Robert W. Rosenberg, "Constituency, Party, and Representation in Congress," *Public Opinion Quarterly* 48 (1984): 741-756.

34. Morris Fiorina, *Divided Government,* 2nd ed., (Boston: Allyn and Bacon, 1996); John W. Kingdon, *Congressmen's Voting Decisions*, 3rd ed. (Ann Arbor: University of Michigan Press, 1989); Richard F. Fenno, *Home Style* (Boston: Little, Brown and Company, 1978).

35. Anthony Downs, *An Economic Theory to Democracy* (New York: Harper, 1957).

36. Michael Bailey and David W. Brady, "Heterogeneity and Representation: The Senate and Free Trade," *American Journal of Political Science* 42 (1998): 524-544.

37. Louis A. Froman, *Congressmen and Their Constituencies* (Chicago: Rand McNally, 1963).

38. Bailey and Brady (1998).

39. Page et al. (1984).

40. E. Scott Alder, "Constituency Characteristics and the 'Guardian' Model of Appropriations Subcommittees 1959-1998," *American Journal of Political Science* 44 (2000): 104-114; W. Wayne Shannon, *Party, Constituency and Congressional Voting* (Baton Rouge: LSU Press, 1968); Aage Clausen, *How Congressmen Decide: A Policy Focus* (New York: St. Martin's Press, 1973); Page et. al (1984).

41. George Edwards, *Presidential Influence in Congress* (San Francisco: W.H. Freeman and Company, 1980), pp. 108-110.

42. Barbara Sinclair, "House Majority Party Leadership in an Era of Divided Control," *Congress Reconsidered*, 5th ed., Lawrence Dodd and Bruce Oppenheimer eds., pp. 237-258 (Washington: CQ Press, 1993); Steven Smith, "Forces of Change in Senate Party Leadership and Organization," *Congress Reconsidered*, 5th ed., Lawrence Dodd and Bruce Oppenheimer eds., pp. 259-290 (Washington: CQ Press, 1993).

43. Allen Schick, "A Surplus, If We Can Keep It," *The Brookings Review* 18 (2000): 36-39.

44. Rubin (2003).

45. Schick (2000).

46. Patrick Fisher, "In the Black: Explanations for the Federal Budget Surplus," *Social Science Journal* 40 (2003): 49-63.

Chapter 2

The Politics of Taxing and Spending

Congressional Spending

Today, only 25% of the budget is considered "controllable" through the budget process. About 77% of uncontrollable expenditures are directed towards entitlements. Some of these entitlement payment levels, such as for unemployment insurance, are very difficult to predict while others, such as Social Security, are fairly predictable. The other 23% of uncontrollable expenditures are directed towards the obligation undertaken by the government when entering into multi-year contract (the lead time for the production of military hardware, for example). Multi-year budgeting can limit the ability of Congress to maneuver in adopting the budget–Congress may not be given the flexibility it needs. Since most government expenditures are disbursed in long-term authorizations, there is some question about the democratic accountability of the budget process.[1]

Another problem with the proliferation of uncontrollable expenditures is the uncertainty of economic projections. The economy drives the budget. The assumptions on which the budget's prescriptions are based all lie at the mercy of national economic conditions. Politics and economics combine to shape the varying patterns of activity for the legislators working on the budget.[2] On the one hand, economic goal-setting has often been a frivolous exercise in symbolic politics in the absence of realistic means to achieve goals. Year after year, the most important factor in determining the current year's budget allocations is last year's budget allocations. On the other hand, the establishment of inflexible methods to achieve a goal may simply make other problems worse and threaten the economy.[3] As economic conditions change, so do priorities; legislators need to maintain their ability to respond to varying economic conditions. By putting much of the budget off limits, Congress is unable to cope with changing economic and political demands.

Growth of Government Spending

Traditionally, congressional budgeting has been seen as an incremental process. Except in extraordinary times (war, depression), budgetary changes were small and at the margins. Incrementalism reduces the chance of unexpected surprises, and even though it does not rule out the possibility of major changes, it prevents major alterations in the budget from occurring quickly. Most decisions are not made by fully rational, total information processes. Rather, the whole policy-making process is dependent upon small incremental decisions that tends to be made in response to short-term political considerations.[4] As a result, today's budget is the result of decisions made years ago and today's budget decisions will affect budgets many years from now.

Incrementalism asserts that budget makers cannot and should not try to reexamine each item every year. As mentioned previously, the largest determining factor of this year's budget is last year's budget. Many items are standard and simply renewed every year unless there is a special reason to challenge them. Thus, a budget is based on the previous budget, with special attention given to a narrow range of increases or decreases. Incrementalism may work well to describe budgeting on an annual basis, but it does not adequately explain the rapid growth of government in the United States this century.

As the scope of government has expanded during the twentieth century, so necessarily has government spending. During the nineteenth century the public sector grew, but it was growing less rapidly than national income. The twentieth century, on the other hand, has been characterized by an increasing governmental share in the national economy.[5] The federal government now spends more than $1 trillion each year, an amount greater than one-fifth of the GNP. Adjusted for inflation, federal outlays are now ten times greater than they were before World War II, four times greater than their postwar level, and two times greater than the 1970 level.[6]

Due to the prevailing consensus that a powerful central government should be avoided, the Founding Fathers designed a federal government that was limited in scope. As a result, federal activities were restricted to traditional public good functions. Due to its restricted role, the federal government consumed only a small and fairly constant share of the economy until the Civil War. Demobilization after the Civil War ended led federal expenditures to drop quickly to a level where they were maintained until World War I. Though with World War I expenditures rose to unprecedented heights, government spending declined sharply as military expenses were cut back, as with the post-Civil War period.[7]

The turning point in the rise of government spending was the Great Depression, as the nation turned to massive federal programs to pull the economy out of the depression. New Deal legislation initiated one program after another to provide jobs and income assistance to those in need. Prior to the 1930s, three-fourths of federal peacetime expenditures were directly related to expense for the military, veterans, and interest on war-related debt.

Three major developments altered the role of the federal government in public finance fiscal policies and affected the allocation of national income in the 1930s. One development was the adoption of Keynesian Economics, which provided theoretical justification for deficit spending and the abandonment of the balanced budget tradition.[8] Another development of the 1930s was the beginning of the federal government's redistribution of income from one group of Americans to another, from one region to another, and from one set of institutions to another. For the first time, federal officials began to influence the distribution of wealth significantly. Finally, the New Deal era also saw the beginning of the gradual development of entitlement programs that benefit all Americans more or less equally, such as Social Security. World War II pushed federal spending to new levels, and even though military spending declined sharply at the end of the war, defense expenditures remained considerably above prewar levels because of the Cold War. Since the 1950s, spending increases have been due to new domestic functions that have been assumed by the federal government.

Why has government taken on new domestic responsibilities, resulting in a dramatic increase in expenditures? There are four potential explanations for the growth of government spending in the twentieth century: 1) Wagner's law; 2) the international economy explanation; 3) the supply-side explanation; and 4) the party control explanation.

Wagner's Law suggests that the rise of government expenditures is largely driven by changes in society, particularly those of industrialization and urbanization. As a society becomes more urbanized, the changes in societal norms (i.e., society becomes much more impersonal) lead to the greater potential for conflict and inequality, which in turn causes government to take on more responsibilities. The international explanation argues that as trade and international investments increase, so does the need for government to play an active role in the nation's economy. The more the nation's economy becomes intertwined with other nations, the greater the pressures on government. The supply-side explanation is based on the belief that as a society modernizes, economic activity becomes easier to detect. Because it is easier to detect who has wealth, the nature of business transactions, etc., it is easier for the government to find and extract money from its citizens. Finally, the party control explanation rests on the premise that spending will rise when a liberal, or pro-government expansion of responsibility, party (the Democratic Party) controls the government and will decline (or will at least not grow as rapidly) when a conservative (or anti-government) party (the Republican Party) is in charge.

In an empirical analysis of these four potential explanations, there was empirical support only for Wagner's Law, and even its support was not unequivocal.[9] This suggests that the causes for the growth of government are much more complex than any of these single-factor explanations would have us believe.

The aforementioned explanations are called "responsive"–they view government as reacting to external demands for public sector activity. The institutions of government are seen as neutral with respect to choice outcomes, and affect the size of the public sector only to the extent that they faithfully reflect the external demands. On the other hand, "excessive" explanations view the choices that institutions of government make as fundamental to understanding the growth of the public sector. In other words, the demand for expansion is conceived as internal to government through a variety of mechanisms such as public employee block voting or "fiscal illusions" that mislead the public into underestimating the costs of public services.[10] It has been argued that citizens fail to estimate properly their true tax costs because the people who pay taxes do not realize how much they pay relative to the governmental services they receive. Government growth, accordingly, is the result of basic bureaucratic influences in democratic decisions.[11] In other words, agency bureaucrats and supporters of public agencies have so much political power that they are able to maintain or increase government spending even though this is not necessarily what the public as a whole wants.

On the other hand, others have claimed that spending produces benefits that are not appreciated by voters because many government benefits are remote compared with taxes and private benefits. Thus, government spending is neither responsive nor excessive. Since citizens are rationally ignorant of remote political events, they fail to comprehend all the government benefits they are receiving.[12] The actual budget a government enacts will be smaller than the "correct" budget because even indirect taxation is much more apparent than many remote government benefits.[13]

The Growth of Entitlements

Entitlements are government spending programs for which Congress has set eligibility criteria–age, income, location, occupation, etc. If a recipient meets the criteria, he or she is "entitled" to the money. While Congress cannot control levels of eligibility in the population, it can control such levels under the law (cost of living adjustments, for example). Entitlements are available for a vote, but only if Congress decides to arrange one. Congress can change or repeal any law it passes, and lawmakers can revisit entitlements at any time to reduce or eliminate them.

Federal entitlement programs range from gigantic ones, such as Social Security and Medicare, to extremely small ones, such as an indemnity program for dairy farmers whose milk is contaminated by chemicals. While most entitlements go to people, some also go to other units of government. The Title XX Social Services block grant, for instance, goes to states based on population. What makes entitlements different from the other major form of congressional spending is that they are mandatory; money must be provided until the program is changed by Congress. By contrast, discretionary spending is good only for one year, and Congress has to renew it annually through the appropriations process.

There are good policy reasons for entitlement spending. Entitlements can be an efficient way of the government providing services, and it seems logical that the government may want to avoid the political difficulty of not being able to maintain its promises regardless of the financial condition of the government, which is, after all, highly reliant on the state of the economy. One problem with entitlements is that, to a large degree, they go to fund what has been called "middle-class

Figure 2.1
Federal Budget Expenditures in 1960 and 2000

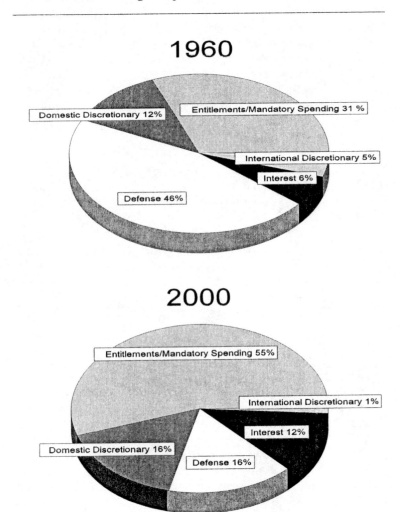

Source: Congressional Budget Office

welfare." That is, entitlement benefits are dispensed largely on the basis of criteria other than income (such as age). Programs that require proof of low income to receive benefits are a small proportion of entitlements. The rapid growth of entitlements has also given them a bad name because they are held to blame for deficits.[14] Furthermore, entitlements came to be seen as a means by which the authorization committees could circumvent the appropriations committees. "Entitlements," according to one prominent budget scholar, "taken together, without a corresponding willingness to raise taxes, broke the back of classical budgeting."[15]

Less than a third of the budget during the Kennedy administration, mandatory spending is now more than one-half of the budget (see Figure 2.1). The huge surge in mandatory spending came between 1966 and 1976. During this period, the creation of programs such as Medicare, Medicaid, and food stamps combined with expanded Social Security benefits to provide an enormous boost to entitlement spending. From 1966-1976, entitlements more than doubled in relation to the size of the economy, growing from 5.4 percent of the Gross Domestic Product (GDP) to 11.3 percent, where it leveled off until health care costs began driving entitlement costs up again in the 1990s.[16] As a percentage of the GDP, discretionary spending is less than half of what it was in 1962, while mandatory spending as a percentage of the GDP has more than doubled (see Figure 2.2).

Anxiety over entitlement spending can be found across the political spectrum. Conservatives fear that the result of the growth in entitlements will be higher taxes and deficits; liberals fear that entitlements will squeeze out other programs and, if they keep growing, use up future revenue increases.[17] Yet both conservatives and liberals in Congress have been unwilling to confront the growth in entitlements. As a result, as Social Security has been placed politically out of reach and other entitlements get harder to contain, discretionary spending has become a larger part of what is up for grabs in the short term.

Some argue that the difficulty in reducing or eliminating entitlements is exactly what the architects of entitlements had intended, and exactly what contemporary Congresses ought to be doing. Entitlement programs dole out benefits automatically so that basic benefits would not be subject to the year-to-year inconsistencies of the appropriations process. Furthermore, entitlements have grown as they were supposed to, especially during a bad economy. The so-called automatic stabilizers such as unemployment insurance and food stamps are designed to pick up the slack during bad economic periods.[18]

Figure 2.2
Major Components of Spending, 1962-2002
(Percentage of GDP)

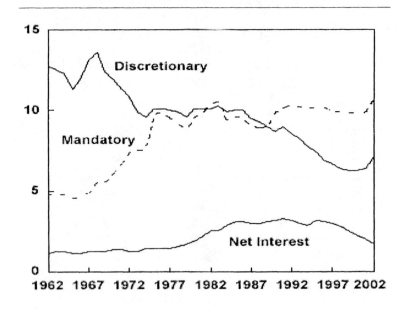

Source: Congressional Budget Office

Entitlement programs, however, do not always have the effect that their creators intended. Times change, but often established entitlements are unable to change as new circumstances dictate. A problem with entitlements is that it is much easier to start an entitlement for an apparently needy group than it is to terminate an entitlement after it no longer makes sense. Most subsidy programs, for example, began for the same reason as programs to benefit individuals–that is, they were a response to hardship cases. In their early days, aid was targeted on the basis of an immediate need or a significant national purpose. Over the years, many of these programs, especially in agriculture, lost their focus as conditions changed. Instead of being phased out, many were expanded for political purposes.[19]

Table 2.1
The Top Entitlement Programs in the United States

Rank	Program	Expenditures	% of GDP
1.	Social Security	406.0	4.1
2.	Medicare	216.0	2.2
3.	Medicaid	117.4	1.2
4.	Other Retirement/Disability	87.8	0.9
5.	Farm Price Supports	30.5	0.3
6.	Unemployment	20.7	0.2
	Total Means Tested	235.9	2.4
	Total Non-Means Tested	793.9	8.1

Dollar amounts in billions
Source: Congressional Budget Office, figures for 2000

Some of the largest and most expensive programs in the federal budget are entitlements such as Social Security and Medicare (see Table 2.1). Politically, these programs are also among the most hazardous to alter. Social Security, in fact, is called by politicians "the third rail of American politics"–touch it and die. Social Security has been remarkably successful at its goal–reducing poverty among the aged. Since the 1930s, however, the group of the popular at greatest risk of poverty has come to be children.[20] Given a choice, members of Congress would rather look almost anywhere else for ways to cut spending. Yet, the cost Social Security and Medicare is rising so fast that they risk crowding out the rest of domestic spending. The political power of Social Security was demonstrated with a House vote in 1994 that called for attacking the deficit by reining in entitlement spending, but with a provision excluding Social Security from any cuts. A move to keep Social Security on the chopping block along with other entitlement programs lost by a resounding vote of 392-37. After this vote the House then proceeded to vote 424-0 to prohibit any move to increase the Social Security payroll tax to help fill the gap in case entitlement spending ever exceeds pre-set limits.[21] Social Security and Medicare are extremely popular programs, but it is now evident that the programs will not be able to sustain themselves without fundamental reforms as the population grows older and more and more Americans qualify for Social Security and Medicare.

The problem remains, however, that it is questionable whether or not the deficit can be successfully attacked without further curbing Social Security. Social Security is the largest single spending program in the federal budget, costing of $406 billion in 2000, accounting for 22 cents out of every dollar the federal government spends.[22] Defenders claim that it should remain as it is because it is self-financed by the payroll tax, which is currently running a huge surplus. A problem with this argument is that it leaves the mistaken impression that the biggest program in the budget would not affect the rest of the budget. Critics argue that the sheer size of Social Security makes it a must for any sizeable budget cuts. As the size of the House votes show, however, any meaningful cuts in Social Security in the near future are unlikely.

Medicare's political power was demonstrated after Congress passed the new Medicare Catastrophic Coverage Act, which was to be paid for in large part by an income surtax on middle- and high-income beneficiaries. After ugly demonstrations lead by those who were going to have to pay the surtax, however, Congress backed down and repealed the measure.[23] Despite Congress' experience with the Catastrophic Coverage Act, the fact still remains that entitlements cannot be controlled ignoring Medicare and Medicaid, the two programs growing faster than any other. It is doubtful, however, that Medicare and Medicaid can be controlled without overhauling the nation's entire heath system.

Taken together, Medicare (the federal health insurance for the elderly and disabled) and Medicaid (the joint federal-state health program for the poor) are almost as expensive as Social Security. Soon after the turn of the century, the two major health programs of the federal government will be larger than Social Security, even though many Americans are left with no health insurance at all.[24] The reason for this is the fact that Medicare and Medicaid are currently by far the fastest growing entitlements. Medicaid alone cost $216 billion in 2000. Medicare and Medicaid have been growing at a tremendous rate both because of demographics and technology. Demographically, health costs increase as Americans get older; the elderly consume far more health-care services than younger people. Medical technology makes health costs more expensive because it provides doctors and hospitals with more things they can do for patients. Thus, not only are our health costs skyrocketing, but the rising costs are not helping to cover those who need health care the most.

Entitlement spending has completely changed the nature of the congressional budget process. The transformation of federal budgeting from a control process to one oriented toward entitlement spending has upset the relationship between available resources and demands on the budget.[25] Claims on the budget became stronger when budgeting was an expansionary process, and it has not been easy for Congress to reverse course as the climate has become more constrained.[26]

Controlling entitlement spending has been more difficult due to the practice of indexing entitlement spending according to rates of inflation. Indexation was initiated at a time when low inflation meant low automatic adjustments and high economic growth meant that resources would be relatively plentiful. Yet it was implemented under conditions in which inflation was high, growth low, and the budget faced large deficits.[27] Beginning in the early 1970s, demands on the budget soared more than resources did. Congress did not foresee in the 1960s that the budget situation would become much more dire as the economy stagnated.

When the budget is squeezed, the easiest place to formulate budget cuts is in the "discretionary spending" portion of the budget, so-named because Congress has, legally speaking, absolute discretion to spend it or not every year through the legislative appropriations process. Discretionary spending includes the choices Congress has to fund state-local assistance and federal domestic programs which cover the spectrum of services–discretionary spending represents the money Congress appropriates every year for everything from battleships to Head Start. The constitutional authority that allows Congress to make annual appropriations, however, is getting weaker by the moment.

The sector of government that Congress can readily get to from one year to another is no longer expanding; in fact, in the 1990s, it has actually been shrinking in real terms. Congress put strict limits on appropriations beginning in 1990 and discretionary spending was kept virtually flat through the rest of this century. This means that there will not be enough money to cover the same value of services the government now provides, much less expand them.[28] Though some of the programs that will be cut may have undoubtedly outlived their usefulness, the decline of discretionary spending will also sacrifice the capacity of Congress to build new programs appropriate to our national needs. This is problematic because even though Americans traditionally have sought to limit government's power, Americans have also continued to demand much from government.[29]

Cutting Spending

The difficulty Congress faces in raising taxes would not be so troublesome if it were not for the trouble it also has in reducing spending. The incentives for Congress to cut spending are weak due, in part, to the perception that cuts alienate voters and, in part, to the inability of Congress to agree on what programs should be eliminated. Members of Congress are more willing to increase spending over committee recommendations than to reduce it when voting on individual expenditure programs. But when members of Congress face votes on explicit economic policy, for example an across-the-board cut in federal spending (which is possibly the worst way to reduce spending because it does not differentiate between good and bad programs), they are more likely to fear connection with the macroeconomic effects.[30] Without the ability to reduce or eliminate individual spending programs, however, Congress is unlikely to be able to come to a meaningful and stable reduction in spending.

Theoretically, Congress should be able to reduce budgets in the same way that they have grown. But subtracting is not the same as adding. In order to reduce spending, it is necessary to establish mechanisms that will force consideration of automatic decisions, set binding ceilings limiting permissible claims, and make choices that will prevent budget run-arounds. Spending cuts eat into the base of existing programs, leading to greater conflict as more and more existing commitments are attacked.[31] To cut, expectations have to be changed, and the capacity to ration resources must be increased.[32]

Budgets are difficult to cut not only because of the rigidities of the decision process, but also because they often constitute long-term commitments to key individuals and groups. The result is that not all areas of the budget are equally susceptible to cuts. In practice, budget cutting tends to concentrate on the controllable parts of the budget and to inflict losses on the politically weaker sections of society (i.e., food stamps, welfare programs, foreign aid, etc.). Ultimately, the politics of subtraction is limited by its social and economic consequences.[33]

Since the advantage of budget cuts lie in accumulating them so as to produce a balanced budget, deals of any kind require people who agree sufficiently to come to a compromise.[34] Because such deals are difficult to bring about, the political process has resulted in only a few terminations of programs because of resistance by Congress, the White House, interest groups, and administrative agencies. Since Congress has found itself unable to make specific cuts in areas in which it is widely acknowledged that cuts need to be made, it has found itself delegating authority to independent commissions, such as a commission which determined military-base closures, to make the cuts it agrees needs to be implemented but which its members do not have the political will to do.

As a result of the federal government's difficulty in cutting expenditures, Congress has turned to innovative means by which to reduce expenditures, including tax legislation. Despite the notion that government writes tax legislation to finance expenditures, recent actions suggest that it has been used to curtail expenditures as well. Tax legislation to control spending is conventionally based on the belief that spending will increase to consume all revenue–the more government has, the more it spends. So by reducing the Treasury's resources, spending must decrease.[35] The problem with this strategy is that since it is much easier to reduce taxes than cut back on spending, tax revenues will drop much more than spending will be limited, creating large deficits. Some, such as Senator D. Patrick Moynihan (D-NY), have suggested that this was exactly the strategy of the Reagan administration's tax cuts in 1981. By reducing tax revenue, it left the United States with unprecedented peace-time deficits that limited what the federal government could spend in future years.

If budget cuts are a necessity, the problem becomes what should be cut. On this point, Congress has remained divided. There are three broad areas of the budget in which Congress can reduce spending: 1) defense, 2) entitlements; and, 3) discretionary spending. In regards to defense, it is questionable how much can be cut in the foreseeable future. Even though the Reagan defense buildup in the 1980s was substantial, defense spending in the 1980s still was considerably below the pre-Vietnam War 1960s.[36] From the end of the Cold War in 1990 until the terrorist attacks of September 11, 2001, defense had been the easiest part of the budget to cut. Even with the defense cuts of the 1990s, however, critics argue that the United States still pays too much on the military. As Table 2.2 shows, the United States spends far more on the military than any other country. From a parochial perspective, however, one problem with cutting defense is that many members of Congress fear that jobs will be lost in their districts. As a result of military cuts in the 1990s, over 300,000 jobs were lost.

Rather than cutting defense, some support greater cuts in entitlements, the fastest growing part of the budget. Should entitlement programs for senior citizens, for example, automatically enjoy a privileged place in the budget? As the populations benefitting most from the

Table 2.2
Top 10 Countries in Military Expenditures
(in billions of dollars)

United States	281
China	89
Japan	43
France	39
United Kingdom	37
Russia	35
Germany	33
Italy	24
Saudi Arabia	21
Taiwan	15

Source: State Department of the United States, figures for 1999

changes in federal spending have grown so has their political leverage in the budget process.[37] Critics of Social Security argue that times have changed since 1935, when it first became law–there are now fewer workers per retired person, and life expectancy has increased dramatically. Social Security now takes up about 13 percent of American workers' paychecks. Proposals for cutting Social Security include: 1) reducing the indexing that is keeping its benefits up with the cost of living; 2) increase taxes on Social Security income; and, 3) raise the age of retirement. Advocating any of these, however, has proven to be politically unpopular and members of Congress, even conservative Republicans, have usually shied away from introducing measures which change the nature of Social Security benefits dramatically.

The other way to reduce spending is to cut discretionary spending through the annual appropriations process. Cutting non-defense discretionary spending may be justified on the grounds that the program is a luxury that we no longer can afford–it is a program that we might want, but not one that we need. The Supercollider is an example of a program that Congress voted to terminate funding for because it was seen as simply too expensive for its perceived benefits in an era of budget constraints.

A part of discretionary spending that might prove to be politically attractive for Congress to cut is grants to the states and local governments. It might be tempting for a federal government that is running large budget deficits to simply leave state and local governments with greater financial responsibilities. The practice of reducing aid to lower levels of governments has already been tried in Canada and Australia as a means of reducing the national deficit. In both countries, the result was a reduction of revenues and an increase in the deficits of the lower levels of government.[38] Thus, such a maneuver simply transfers more responsibilities to lower levels of government, who are then burdened with the budget problems that Congress now faces. This does not necessarily make for better public policy, but it is one of the easier mechanisms by which Congress can reduce the spending levels of the federal government, even though some of these programs have active, organized clienteles that would fight any cuts.

The fact remains, however, that the parts of the budget that are easiest to control have been cut to the point where few obvious cuts remain.[39]   Cutting spending requires Congress to upset some constituencies, such as the elderly, and this is something that it has been extremely reluctant to do.

Congress and Taxes

The tax side of the budget should be considered equal to the spending side of the budget in its political and economic importance. Many critics of the congressional budget process place the blame for skyrocketing deficits on the inability of Congress to curtail spending.[40] But one can just as easily argue that it is the inability of Congress to tax enough that makes it impossible for our government to balance the budget. It may be that the obstacles the American political system places on raising revenues is what makes Congress look so inadequate at budgeting.

Taxes have been the subject of political controversy since the United States was founded. The Constitution provides in Article I, Section 8 that "the Congress shall have power to lay and collect taxes, duties, imports and excises, to pay the debts and provide for the common defense and general welfare of the United States." This provision represents a sweeping grant of fiscal authority to Congress because it covers almost any common form of taxation imaginable. The constitutional framers, fearing potential abuses of executive branch

Figure 2.3
Federal Budget Revenues in 1960 and 2000

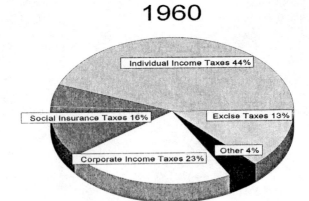

1960

Individual Income Taxes 44%
Social Insurance Taxes 16%
Excise Taxes 13%
Other 4%
Corporate Income Taxes 23%

2000

Individual Income Taxes 50%
Excise Taxes 3%
Other 5%
Corporate Income Taxes 10%
Social Insurance Taxes 32%

Source: Congressional Budget Office

control of the power of the purse, made sure that tax proposals had to be passed by the people's branch of government, the legislative branch, and originate in the House, originally the only political institution elected directly by the public.

Today, individual income taxes and social insurance receipts (mainly from a payroll tax) are the dominant sources of revenue for the federal government. These taxes, however, are relative newcomers as important sources of revenue. From our nation's founding until World War I, tariffs and excise taxes remained the primary source of revenue for the tiny national government. The income tax was unknown until it was used briefly during the Civil War. It then remained unused until 1894, when President Grover Cleveland convinced Congress to lower tariffs and substitute a modest tax on incomes to recoup revenues. The Supreme Court, however, ruled the income tax unconstitutional in *Pollock v. Farmers Loan and Trust* in 1895. As a result, the federal government ran deficits 11 of the 21 years between 1894-1914.[41]

As a reaction to their inability to balance the budget, both Democrats and Republicans in Congress finally rallied behind a constitutional amendment to allow the income tax, and after the provision sped through Congress with little debate it was ratified in 1913. Except for World War I, the income tax remained very small until the New Deal era. In order to pay for New Deal programs and later to help finance World War II, Franklin Roosevelt raised the individual and corporate income taxes to unprecedented levels and introduced the payroll tax to pay for Social Security. Since the end of World War II, the federal tax system has gradually become less progressive. As Figure 2.3 displays, revenue raised from the corporate income tax has declined substantially over the past four decades (from 23 percent of revenues in 1960 to only 10 percent in 2000) while payroll taxes have increased substantially (from 16 percent of revenues in 1960 to 32 percent of revenues in 2000). As a percentage of the GDP, social insurance taxes have more than doubled since 1960, while corporate income taxes are less than half what they were in 1960 (see Figure 2.4). One-quarter of all American households now pay more in Social Security taxes than in income taxes. Since 1990 employers and employees have each paid 7.65 percent of their earned income to finance Social Security and Medicare, 1.45 percent for Medicare and 6.20 percent for Social Security. Self-employed individuals pay both shares–15.3 percent. Workers do not pay social security taxes on wages above $85,000, though they continue to pay the heath insurance tax. As a result, the payroll tax is a far greater burden on

Figure 2.4
Revenues, by Source, as a Share of GDP, 1960-2013

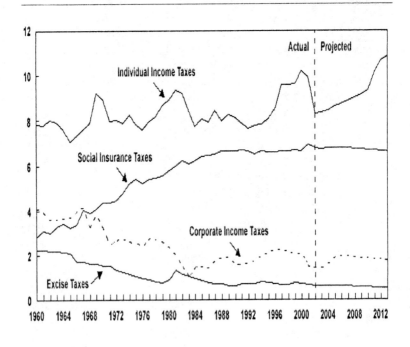

Source: Congressional Budget Office

low-income households than is the income tax.

Taxes have in fact remained fairly steady at about 18-19% of the GDP since the 1950s (see Figure 2.5). The net result of all of the budgetary battles of the last 30 years is that the government's overall tax burden, measured by the share of the GDP it takes through taxes, has stayed almost exactly the same. Yet there has been an important change in the composition of who is paying the taxes. Federal tax rates used to be considerably more progressive than they are today: during World War II, for example, the top income tax rate was an incredible 91%! Thus, for middle-income Americans, the overall tax burden has increased because of the increasing burden of payroll taxes.[42] In political

Figure 2.5
Total Revenues as a Share of GDP, 1946-2013

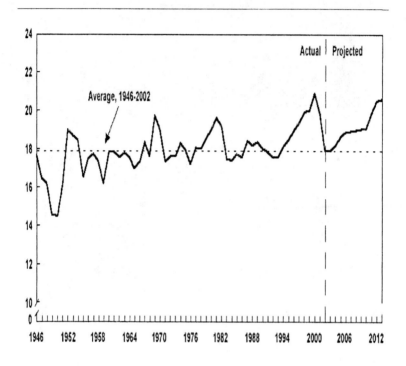

Source: Congressional Budget Office

as well as economic terms, taxes are the cost of providing government benefits. Comparatively peaking, the United States appears to be less willing to pay the costs of these benefits than other countries, as Figure 2.6 demonstrates.

The single biggest difference between the American and European tax systems is the fact that the United States does not have a national consumption tax. In fact, if the United States collected the same average amount of consumption taxes as the European Union (12.7 percent instead of 4.9 percent), it would collect 37.8 percent of the GDP in taxes. In short, if the United States had such a tax, its overall tax rate

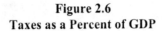

Figure 2.6
Taxes as a Percent of GDP

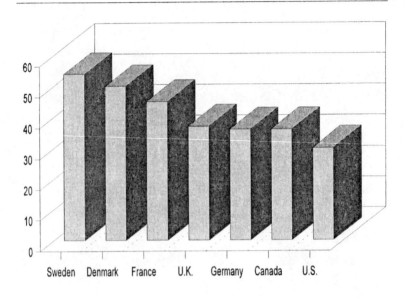

Source: Organization for Economic Cooperation and Development (1998)

would be similar to those of European nations.[43] Sweden, for example, spends more on public policy programs than the United States because the Social Democratic Party in Sweden has been able to build a tax system that is very broadly based and efficient. It is not necessarily a lack of will, but rather the fragmentation of political authority in the United States that has stifled congressional efforts to broaden the tax base and introduce consumption taxes.[44] Whether it is because of the contradictions of citizen demands or due to the inadequacies of the American political system, Congress has found it extraordinarily difficult to raise enough revenues to meet spending demands.

The Politics of Taxing

Americans tend to have contradictory opinions concerning public finance. They tend to deplore government spending in the abstract, but to welcome it for the specific programs that benefit them. The problem members of Congress face is that voters would like more benefits for the same or lower taxes. Citizens generally do not like taxes, but most appear to have come to the realistic acceptance that taxes are both necessary and inevitable. On the whole, they like the benefits they receive from government, and tend to be much more willing to pay taxes when reminded of the benefits received as a consequence of doing so. Majorities are in favor of the same or greater expenditures for programs even once the "tax price" is introduced.[45]

Part of the reason voters have strong negative feelings about federal taxes while also having positive feelings about government services (although not "government" in general) may be that taxpayers have no clear idea for what the money is being spent. Many believe that it is being spent wastefully or even fraudulently, or that a substantial part of it goes for services of which they disapprove.[46] Voters are largely uninformed, but they also tend to be rationally self-interested in many respects. Since benefits are often diffuse, citizens are insensitive or unaware of a large share of benefits they receive, but because taxes are direct, citizens are aware of the costs of government. Also, because public transactions are different from private transactions, people's attitudes toward the two differ. Private transactions are done on a quid pro quo basis: one pays a specific amount for a specific good or service. With most taxes, however, the payment is for services or goods that we do not directly receive. This leaves the impression that taxes are a net loss rather than a payment.[47]

It has been argued that this combination of factors produces an "incorrect" government budget. Since citizens are rationally ignorant of remote political events, they fail to realize all the government benefits they are receiving. The federal budget deficit can thus be explained as the inability of citizens to make the connection between the taxes they pay and the benefits they receive. People want their taxes reduced, but they do not want to have their benefits reduced.

Different people are willing to pay for different public programs. The result is that taxpayers often correctly believe that their taxes pay for something that they do not like. For the political left, taxes pay for too many bombers; for the political right, taxes pay for lazy welfare recipients. Since people feel that they have little control over how money is spent, citizens feel that their tax dollars are being wasted on policies that they oppose.[48] When asked, "If you could be guaranteed that increased government spending would be efficiently and effectively used to address society's problems, would you agree to increase your taxes?," the vast majority answered yes. Respondents, however, do not believe that revenue from higher taxes would be used efficiently or effectively, and therefore they would not approve tax increases given the choice under normal circumstances. Given the way politics works in the United States, people do not trust the system to use the increased tax burden to pay for programs that benefitted those who truly needed help.[49]

Raising Taxes

Members of Congress have created a system that shields them from electoral retribution for raising taxes, but this is not foolproof. The anticipation of retrospective voting helps to focus legislative attention on the possible electoral consequences of voting to raise taxes even when they hear little from their constituents in advance of congressional action.[50] Even though there is little evidence that members of Congress have incurred significant electoral risks for approving new taxes, policymakers fear the potential consequences of raising taxes.[51] The Democrats lost presidential races in 1984 and 1988 in part for even suggesting income tax increases, enhancing the perception that supporting tax increases is a vote loser.

This aversion to risk extends to the type of taxes members of Congress are willing to raise when revenue must be increased. As experiences at the state level have shown, it is much more difficult to impose new taxes than to raise existing ones.[52] This means that Congress tends to refuse to repeal established taxes because of the fear of losing revenue, and at the same time it does not want to introduce new taxes because a new tax can potentially have an unfavorable impact upon the electorate. By making few changes, members of Congress keep past laws in effect as the best means of minimizing the political costs of taxation while maximizing tax revenue.[53] By treating tax policy as a "nondecision" rather than as a matter of legislative choice, informal rules and behavioral patterns assure that a policy already in place will continue in effect without new explicit decisions being made. This is not just inertia, but a systematic bias of Congress against active consideration of aspects of the nation's tax policy.[54]

In order to produce balanced budgets, Congress must overcome the obstacle that garnering support for tax increases is different from gaining support for spending. To gain support for spending, one can build a coalition, either by spreading the money around a little to each group or by promising some program increases this year or in future years. Since members of Congress hope that by going along with spending proposals they might get the support they need in the future, there should be little active opposition to spending. For taxation, however, there is a built-in set of active opponents and no natural support, except perhaps among agency heads. To increase taxes requires major efforts to create support and defuse opposition.[55] In order for legislators to support raising taxes they must either convince the public that there is a dramatic need for a tax increase, or they must prove to citizens that their money will not be wasted. Given people's current opinion of the federal government, the latter is a difficult task indeed.

The need for periodic tax increases is an important link between the taxpayers and the government, keeping government expenditures in line with the desires of the taxpayers. Congress plans very carefully for tax increases. They plan the timing, devise and use processes that insulate them from interest groups, strategize to minimize the pain to voters, and build coalitions of support.[56] Taxes may not be popular, but it impossible for government to exist without them. The problem for our elected representatives in Congress is that voters do not perceive that they receive in benefits what they pay in taxes. At the same time, the voters are not reducing their demands upon government.

Though cutting spending is the most often sought solution by members of Congress to reduce the deficit, it should be remembered that raising taxes is another, if not always politically popular, option. In fact, any realistic attempt at reducing the deficit probably would have to contain increased revenues. Yet if taxpayers perceive that they pay an unfair share of general federal taxes that support vaguely understood and inefficiently produced services, raising taxes becomes a hard sell. It is difficult for policymakers to campaign for higher taxes if most people do not see an increase in the services that government provides them.[57]

Potential sources to increase revenue in the future include: an increased reliance on user fees, an increase of taxes held in trust funds and earmarked for specific purposes, an increase in sin, payroll, energy (gasoline) and/or income taxes, and imposing a national value-added tax (VAT). Of these, the VAT may offer the best potential for significant revenue increases.

Compared to other deficit reduction options, a VAT looks quite attractive. Estimates are that a VAT would raise between $10 billion to $20 billion a year in new revenue for each one percent of tax.[58] The VAT is a type of consumption tax in place in more than 50 countries, including Canada, Japan, and Great Britain. The United States is one of the few Western industrialized nations without a VAT and the only one without either a VAT or national sales tax. The levy is so named because it is imposed on the "value added" at every stage of production or service. A business that spends $10,000 on raw materials and other costs to turn out a product that sell for $15,000 would pay tax on only the $5,000 difference.[59]

Economists tend to like the VAT because by taxing consumption, it would not discourage savings and investment, both of which are subject to the income tax. Though the VAT has attracted theoretical interest in Congress for many years, congressional opposition to such a tax is immense. Liberals object to a VAT because sales taxes are regressive. Conservatives fear the tax is a secret tax that is used in Europe mainly as a device to finance their welfare states. Increasing congressional antipathy toward the VAT is that fact that former chairman of the House Ways and Means Committee, Al Ullman (D-OR), lost his House seat after his advocacy of the tax was made a dominant issue in his 1980 reelection campaign.

Another type of tax increase–closing tax expenditures–would arguably be much less painful for Congress to enact. Tax expenditures are "loopholes" in the tax code that reduce the "normal" tax liability for an individual or a corporation. Critics of tax expenditures argue that these costs and direct spending should be treated equally. As a senior fellow at the Urban Institute argues, "tax expenditures are every bit as much entitlements as those on the spending side."[60] Tax expenditures such as home mortgage interest deductions and net exclusion of pension contributions and earnings constitute huge benefits, much of which are heavily skewed toward the wealthy. Such breaks cost the federal government an estimated $320 billion in foregone revenues in 1992.[61] Many early tax expenditures distributed benefits broadly to most tax payers, but the preferences added to the tax code in recent years have tended to be narrowly distributed to businesses or the wealthy. A backlash against such preferential treatment has lead to numerous proposals of means-testing federal benefits–denying or scaling back benefits over a certain income level.

Given the unpopularity of taxes, it might be taken as an article of faith that cutting federal taxes would be seen as a politically expedient maneuver for members of Congress. The anticipation of retrospective voting helps to focus legislative attention on the possible electoral benefits of voting to cut taxes even when they hear little from their constituents in advance of congressional action. Members of Congress, however, may not be worried so much about the electoral benefits of voting to reduce taxes as much as they fear the negative electoral consequences of voting against tax cuts.

While the electoral sanction may be central to democratic governance, it has been argued that incumbents in the House of Representatives have such advantages that the electorate does not have a meaningful say in who does and does not belong in office.[62] Public opinion may shape the collective behavior of Congress, but at the same time its influence on substantive policy decisions of individual members has been found to be modest. In one study, there was little evidence that public opinion exerted a direct influence on the positions taken by individual legislators.[63] If members of Congress do not fear electoral retribution, then its members may be more likely to make votes on tax policy without considering public opinion.

Individual members of Congress may be able to make potentially unpopular votes on tax policy because they are able to avoid being tarnished by negative impressions of the institution as a whole. While the standing of Congress as an institution is low, the approval ratings of individual members is not.[64] There is a disassociation between the institutional reputation of Congress and the reelection prospects of its members; people tend to dislike Congress as an institution while supporting their own representative. These seemingly contradictory attitudes are the result of what Americans have come to expect of their legislative representatives. As it is now organized, Congress tends to serve the political interests of individual members well, but not necessarily the interests of the institution as a whole.[65] This is the so-called legislature-legislator dichotomy, in which appraisals of individual members are perceived to be independent of those characteristics of the institution of Congress as a whole. As it turns out, members of Congress may be vastly overestimating their own invulnerability to the negative impressions constituents hold of the institution as a whole.

Tax Policy With the Advent of Budget Surpluses

The large budget deficits that resulted after the Congress passed the income tax cuts proposed by President Reagan in 1981 hindered further efforts to reduce income tax rates. The tremendous size of the budget deficits of the 1980s and early 1990s had congressional Republicans on the defensive: for the most part they were trying to prevent income taxes from being raised in the name of deficit reduction. After Bill Clinton was elected president, a Democratic majority in Congress did manage to increase income tax rates, though just barely (the vote won without a vote to spare in either the House or the Senate), with the passage of the 1993 Budget Reconciliation Bill. When the Republicans took control of Congress after the 1994 elections, they found themselves in a position to once again try to reduce federal tax rates. The size of the deficit, however, limited the Republicans ability to do so and to a large degree the party focused on cutting spending in an attempt to possibly be able to cut taxes further in the future.

The creation of a federal budget surpluses from 1998-2001, however, totally changed the dynamics of political debate over budget priorities. To illustrate how much the budgetary picture changed from the early part of the 1990s to the latter part of the decade, in 1993 the Congressional Budget Office projected a fiscal 1998 deficit of $357 billion; the actual 1998 fiscal budget had a surplus of $63 billion.[66] Americans who became so accustomed to debates over how to reduce the deficit suddenly faced lawmakers debating how to spend a projected budget surplus. The surplus provided an opportunity for Congress to debate the budgetary priorities of the United States for the 21st century. With the deficit eliminated, it was possible to once again have a debate over whether the federal government should do more or cut taxes.[67] While Democrats tended to support using the surplus to shore up entitlement programs such as Social Security and Medicare, Republicans advocated tax cuts and, in the wake of the terrorist attacks of September 11, 2001, increasing defense spending.

Unleashed from the burden of budget deficits, congressional Democrats and Republicans alike relished the chance to be able to make popular promises. Both parties proposed spending hundreds of billions of dollars over the next decade for purposes that had been neglected in recent years–everything from education to defense–because of the fiscal restraints large budget deficits placed on policymakers. Lawmakers, however, are no where near a consensus on how the extra revenues should be distributed.

Once the federal budget surplus became a reality, the Republican majority in Congress made tax cuts a major feature of their economic agenda. During the 106th Congress (1999-2000), Speaker J. Dennis

Hastert and his deputies proclaimed that they would use budget surpluses not generated by Social Security to give a wide variety of tax breaks. The main elements of the congressional Republican tax bill would reduce income tax rates by one percentage point, lower the capital gains tax, give more favorable tax treatment to retirement savings, gradually abolish the inheritance tax, and give generous tax breaks to a wide variety of commercial interests. Though it was vetoed by President Clinton, at $792 billion over 10 years, the tax reduction approved by Congress was the biggest it had passed since 1981. Congressional Democrats assailed the bill as short-sighted and a boon to the wealthy In lieu of using the surplus for a broad-based tax cuts that Republicans suggested, congressional Democrats sought to use the surplus to pursue many of the goals they had previously abandoned and put on hold and to rally support for his plan to save future surpluses for Social Security and Medicare.

Thus, while Democrats in Congress tended to emphasize using the surplus to protect the future of Social Security and Medicare as well as reducing the national debt, Republicans in Congress were inclined to view the surplus as an opportunity to press for tax cuts, and once a Republican was elected to the presidency the Republican were finally able to pass tax cuts.

Despite the closeness of the 2000 presidential election and the disputed nature of his victory, George W. Bush decided to make cutting taxes the number one priority of his new administration. Bush's plan called for a reduction of all federal income tax rates, raising the child credit, giving a break to married couples and repealing the federal tax on large estates. Overall, the Bush tax plan was expected to reduce federal taxes by $1.6 trillion over ten years.

President Bush argued that his plan to cut taxes would restrain the growth of government spending and provide the money needed to address issues he considered priorities. At the same time, he contended that the projected federal surplus of $5.6 trillion over the next decade made his $1.6 trillion tax cut in the same period affordable. The large surplus, therefore, justified the tax cuts. "The surplus is not the government's money," claimed Bush. "The surplus is the people's money. And I'm here to ask you to join me in making that case to any federal official you can find." Bush also sold the tax cut as a way to shore up the economy, which was showing signs of slowing just as Bush won the presidency. Thus, not only was a tax cut a means by which to return people their own money, it was also antirecession insurance.

After intense negotiations over how to apportion the tax cut, it was decided that the income tax rates would be reduced to 10 percent, 15 percent, 25 percent, 33 percent, and 35 percent, depending on the wealth of the taxpayer. Republican leaders moved the final budget quickly through both the House and the Senate and the bill passed the House by a vote of 240 to 154 and the Senate then passed it by a vote of 58 to 33. Congressional Democrats, no longer able to rely on a veto from the White House to back them up, criticized the bill for being unfairly tilted to the wealthy, leaving too little money for other purposes and risking putting the nation back in the red just as it confronted the costs of paying Social Security and Medicaid to an aging population.

Even though the plan approved by Congress was smaller than the $1.6 trillion plan Bush had originally proposed, the president signed the bill with enthusiasm. President Bush made a big tax cut the centerpiece of his economic agenda and his first legislative priority and was now able to declare victory. The passage of the tax cuts was the culmination of years of debate over whether the nation could afford a substantial tax reduction at a time of large and growing federal budget surpluses. Not only was the passage of the tax cuts a victory for Bush, but it was also a victory for Republicans in Congress, who had been thwarted in their tax-cutting efforts while Clinton was in the White House.

Conclusion

The most important constraint on congressional budgeting is the desire to balance revenues and expenditures. Both the public and the financial community oppose deficits. Since the 1940s, opinion polls have shown that the public overwhelmingly favors balanced budgets.[68] Since deficits are embarrassing, Congress tries to minimize their size and importance, as demonstrated by the games that are played with the budget numbers. Because the idea of a balanced budget is so popular, it has been difficult for members of Congress to take stands that are directly opposed to the concept of balancing the budget.

Since the 1960s, however, budgeting has become much more difficult because much of what the government does—income for the elderly, providing health care, national defense—has become far more expensive. At the same time, strong antitax feelings have made raising more money to pay for these programs increasingly difficult.[69]

As a result, the balanced-budget norm can no longer constrain and coordinate decisions as it had in the past. The result has been the rise in partisanship in Congress over the ideal of a balanced budget. Since

Democrats and Republicans alike tend to argue, at least in the abstract, that the budget should be balanced, the aim of balancing the budget is not necessarily a partisan issue. The means by which to balance the budget, however, is a very partisan issue. Balancing the budget requires difficult compromises. Both sides have to realize that they will not get everything they want.

Endnotes

1. Aaron Wildavsky and Naomi Caiden, *The New Politics of the Budgetary Process*, 4th edition (New York: Longman, 2001).

2. Richard Fenno, *The Emergence of a Senate Leader: Pete Domenici and the Reagan Budget* (Washington, DC: CQ Press, 1991).

3. Lance Leloup, "Fiscal Policy and Congressional Politics," *Congressional Politics*, Christopher Deering ed., pp. 262-283 (Pacific Grove, CA: Brooks/Cole, 1989), p. 281.

4. Charles Lindbloom, "The Science of Muddling Through," *Public Administration Review* 39 (1959): 517-526.

5. James Buchanan, "Why Does Government Grow?," *Budgets and Bureaucrats: The Sources of Government Growth*, Thomas Borcherding ed., pp. 3-18 (Durham, NC: Duke University Press, 1977).

6. Allen Schick, *The Capacity to Budget* (Washington, D.C.: The Urban Institute, 1990), p. 15.

7. Donald Ogilvie, "Constitutional Limits and the Federal Budget," *The Congressional Budget Process After Five Years*, Ruldolph Penner, ed., pp. 101-134 (Washington, D.C.: AEI), pp. 103-104.

8. John Maynard Keynes, *The General Theory of Employment, Interest, and Money* (Harcourt Brace Jovanovich: New York, 1937).

9. David Lowery and William Berry, "The Growth of Government in the United States: An Empirical Assessment of Competing Explanations," *American Journal of Political Science* 27 (1983): 665-694.

10. William Berry and David Lowery, "Explaining the Size of the Public Sector: Responsive and Excessive Government Interpretations," *Journal of Politics* 49 (1987): 401-440.

11. Buchanan (1977), pp. 7-18.

12. Anthony Downs, "Why the Government is Too Small in a Democracy," *World Politics* 12 (1960): 541-563.

13. Ibid., p. 559.

14. Dennis Ippolito, *Why Budgets Matter: Budget Policy and American Politics* (University Park: Pennsylvania State University Press, 2003).

15. Wildavsky and Caiden (2001), p.195.

16. George Hager. "Entitlements: The Untouchable May Become the Unavoidable," *Congressional Quarterly*, January 2, 1993, pp. 22-30.

17. Wildavsky and Caiden (2001).

18. Ibid.

19. Glenn Pascall, *The Trillion Dollar Budget* (Seattle: University of Washington Press, 1985), p. 264.

20. Donald F. Kettl, *Deficit Politics* (New York: Longman, 2003), p. 60.

21. George Hager. "Social Security Still Untouchable as House Targets Entitlements," *Congressional Quarterly*, July 23, 1994, p. 2020.

22. Ibid.

23. Hager, "Entitlements: The Untouchable May Become Unavoidable" (1993), p. 26.

24. Ruldolph Penner, "Federal Spending Issues of the 1990s," *Balancing Act*, John Makin, Norman Ornstein and David Zlowe eds., pp. 63-88 (Washington, D.C.: AEI, 1990).

25. Ippolito (2003).

26. Allen Schick, *The Capacity to Budget* (Washington, DC: Urban Institute, 1990), pp. 8-12.

27. Ibid., chapter 2.

28. George Hager. "A New Dynamic," *Congressional Quarterly* Dec. 11, 1993, pp. 6-11.

29. Kettl (2003), p. 45.

30. R. Douglas Arnold, *The Logic of Congressional Action* (New Haven: Yale University Press, 1990) pp. 171-172.

31. Naomi Caiden, "The Politics of Subtraction," *Making Economic Policy in Congress*, Allen Schick, ed., pp. 100-130 (Washington, D.C.: AEI, 1983), p. 103.

32. Schick (1990), p. 85.

33. Ibid., p. 128.

34. Wildavsky and Caiden (2001), p. 169.

35. Ibid., p. 137.

36. Kettl (2003), p. 48.

37. Ibid., p. 168.

38. General Accounting Office, *Deficit Reduction: Experiences of Other Countries* (Washington, D.C.: U.S. Government Press, 1994), p. 44.

39. Kettl (2003), p. 157.

40. Dennis Ippolito, *Congressional Spending* (Ithaca: Cornell University Press, 1981); Joseph White and Aaron Wildavsky *The Deficit and the Public Interest* (Berkeley: University of California Press, 1989); Schick (1990); Wildavsky and Caiden (2001).

41. Wildavsky and Caiden (2001), pp. 55-56.

42. Ibid., pp.72-73.

43. Sven Steinmo, *Taxation and Democracy* (New Haven: Yale University, 1993), p. 196.

44. Ibid.

45. Guy Peters, *The Politics of Taxation* (Cambridge, MA: Blackwell, 1991), pp. 187-188.

46. Alice Rivlin, "The Continuing Search for a Popular Tax" *AEA Papers and Proceedings* (Washington, D.C.: AEI, 1989).

47. Steinmo (1993), pp. 193-194.

48. Ibid., p. 194.

49. Ibid., pp. 199-200.

50. Arnold (1990), p. 194.

51. Ibid.

52. Susan Hansen, "Extraction: The Politics of State Taxation," *Politics in the American States*, Virginia Gray, Herbert Jacob, and Kenneth Vines, eds. (Glenview, IL: Scott, Foresman, and Company, 1983).

53. Richard Rose, "Maximizing Tax Revenue While Minimizing Political Costs," *Journal of Public Policy* 5 (1986): 289-320, p. 307.

54. Allen Schick, *Congress and Money* (Washington, D.C.: AEI, 1980), p. 483.

55. Irene Rubin, *The Politics of Public Budgeting* (Chatham, NJ: Chatham House, 1990), p. 30.

56. Ibid., p. 39.

57. Kettl (2003), p. 162.

58. Robert Lee and Ronald Johnson, *Public Budgeting Systems*, 5th edition (Gaithersbueg: MD: Aspen Publishers, 1994), p. 70.

59. David Cloud, "VAT Would Bring Big Revenue, but Prospects Slim on Hill," *Congressional Quarterly* (April 24, 1993), pp. 1005-1006.

60. Hager (1993), "Entitlements: The Untouchable May Become Unavoidable," p. 30.

61. Ibid.

62. Everett Carll Ladd , "Public Opinion and the 'Congress Problem,'" *The Public Interest* 100 (1990): 57-67.

63. Lawrence R. Jacobs, Eric D. Lawrence, Robert Y. Shapiro, and Steven S. Smith, "Congressional Leadership on Public Opinion," *Political Science Quarterly* 113 (1998): 21-41.

64. Kelley D. Patterson and David B. Magleby, "Public Support for Congress," *Public Opinion Quarterly* 56 (1992): 539-551.

65. Richard F. Fenno, *Home Style* (Boston: Little, Brown and Company, 1978).

66. Allen Schick, "A Surplus, If We Can Keep It," *The Brookings Review* 18 (2000): 36-39.

67. E.J. Dionne, "Why Americans Hate Politics: A Reprise," *The Brookings Review* 18 (2000): 8-11.

68. Rubin (1990), chapter 5.

69. Kettl (2003), p. 157.

Chapter 3

The Institutional Dynamics of Congressional Budgetary Decisions

A Madisonian Budget Process

Budgeting is the single most important decision-making process for the government. Almost all political issues eventually become budgetary issues.[1] The budget sets the priorities for the nation and is the government's most important contemporary political document at any point in time. It sets forth the massive dollar benefits that flow from the federal government to every individual and interest group in the country. The emergence of formal governmental budgeting can be traced to a concern for holding public officials accountable for their actions. In a democracy, budgeting is a process for limiting the powers of government.[2]

Budgeting for the United States is an extremely difficult undertaking. The budget process can be called Madisonian because it is designed less to secure efficiency than to prevent abuse of power.[3] Americans are taught in school James Madison's arguments that "separation of powers" and "checks and balances" prevent tyrannical government and protect minorities. These safeguards against democratic excesses, however, have severe drawbacks for budgeting. The budget process of the United States is unique in its complexity. In other countries the executive assembles a budget proposal, and presents it to the legislature, expecting it to pass, as designed, in one bill. The legislature is in no position to extensively revise the executive's plan. No other nation has a legislature so strong that it actually dominates spending and taxing decisions.[4]

For decades Americans have been chronically unhappy with the manner in which the federal budgetary process is run. This unhappiness has lead to seeming endless cries for reform. Since wants and desires are always greater than resources, there will probably always be some voices who will express their dislike of budgets resulting from the process of public finance. Budgetary decisions are, in the end, about scarcity.[5] Unfortunately, the problems of the budgetary process appear to be even more severe today than they have been in the past. The effectiveness of budgeting in the United States has been seriously eroded in recent years, as can be seen by the nation's record deficits. Furthermore, the basic rules of accounting for the budget have apparently broken down.[6] The budgetary process of today is arguably a threat to the future well-being of the United States. The inability of Congress to balance the budget by either restraining spending or increasing revenues has destroyed the traditional norms of budgetary behavior. Lack of consensus plagues the budgetary process; Congress can only control the budget once it decides to compromise on how much for what purpose and who is to pay.

Political dynamics frequently hamper the budget process. The individual career incentives of policymakers are not conducive toward making the difficult budgetary decisions that must be made. Coalitional instability makes it more improbable that varying forces will be able to maintain budgetary agreements. The increasing polarization of the budgetary process in recent years (such as the tendency of the Office of Management and Budget to "cook the books" so that the budget figures are favorable to the President) has become problematic in developing the budget. Politics makes resolving the current problems of the national budget process a difficult, if not impossible, task. Since Congress is faced with the problem that the American citizenry wants more than the government can afford, the process of making the federal budget is plagued by the "where there is a will there is a way" principle.

How Do Members of Congress Make Budgetary Decisions?

It has been said that public budgeting's central premise is: "On what basis shall it be decided to allocate X dollars to activity A instead of activity B?"[7] Congress, as budget maker, never has enough revenue to meet all spending requests; as a result, it must determine how scarce

Figure 3.1
Misestimates in CBO's Projections Made from 1981 to 1997
(Percentage of the GDP)

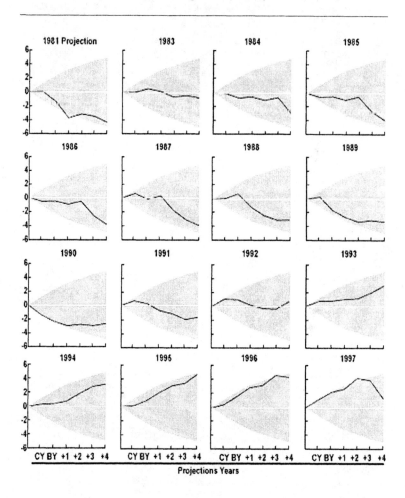

means shall be allocated to alternative uses. As budget maker, Congress has few agreed-upon and universally applicable standards of evaluation. Rather, it acts on the basis of member values and interests. Unfortunately, the relative merit of different values and interests cannot be compared in the absence of a common denominator.

Budgeting, therefore, tends to be an inexact science. This is especially the case when it involves forecasting future needs and conditions.[8] Even short-term budget forecasts can be far off the mark. This can be seen by looking at the projections of the Congressional Budget Office (CBO). As Figure 3.1 displays, the CBO's budget projections have often been far off the mark, with the CBO tending to overestimate future revenues from 1981 to 1992 (during the Reagan and Bush administrations) and underestimating future revenues from 1993 to 1997 (during the Clinton administration). The sometimes dramatic misestimates of the CBO's projections underlines the difficulty members of Congress face when trying to make decisions on the budget.

At the same time, however, the inexact science of budgeting helps members of Congress avoid making politically tough choices, especially those that deal with long-term concerns (such as entitlement reform). If long-term projections are bleak, members of Congress can simply ignore the unfavorable forecasts, arguing that budget forecasts in the past have been wrong and thus they are destined to be wrong in the future.

For most members of Congress, re-election tends to be the overriding goal. The ideal world for legislators is one in which they can make everyone happy and alienate no one. Legislators favor structures that reduce the probability of conflict, promote the routine resolution of disputes, and put distance between themselves and whatever conflicts arise. The congressional budget process is structured in such a way that budget routines and standard operating procedures dominate the proceeding, and these tend to be highly resistant to change.[9]

Members of Congress are faced with the task of how to minimize political costs while maximizing tax revenue. The object is damage limitation or blame-sharing in an era in which it is no longer generally accepted that it is practicable to have "policy without pain." The inertia of established laws minimizes political costs. The great majority of revenue laws are old laws. By sustaining familiar taxes, inertia tends to make taxation politically acceptable, while new tax proposals can induce anxiety by their unfamiliarity.[10] When inertia processes of taxation fail to generate a sufficient amount of revenue to meet expected expenditure,

Congress can resort to borrowing to fund the deficit–what has been called the "non-decisionmaking model." This gets around the need for Congress to make a decision about matters that are both visible and likely to be politically unpopular (i.e., raising taxes or reducing spending). Non-decisionmaking treats borrowing as a continuously desirable political strategy.[11]

The non-decisionmaking model can be seen in the way members of Congress tend to find ways to avoid casting votes that can be used against them in their next election. Over the years, Congress has developed countless techniques to enable its members to dodge tough votes on the budget and deficit. For instance, the House automatically agrees to raise the statutory ceiling on the federal debt when it approves its annual budget resolution. This action avoids what used to be an embarrassing debate and vote that forced representatives to address directly how large the debt had become.

The desire to avoid troublesome votes is most intense when tax increases are at stake. In the Senate, tax issues are often settled by votes to table legislation, where "table" is just another word for "kill." For example, in the debate over the 1993 reconciliation bill, Republicans offered amendments that would have eliminated provisions to raise the tax on gasoline and increase the proportion of Social Security benefits to income taxes. Since those taxes were central to Clinton's budget proposal, the Democrats killed the amendments by voting to table them. That maneuver made it appear as if they were voting on a procedural matter rather than specifically on raising taxes on motorists and the elderly. In the House, tax bills are always considered under what are called closed rules, meaning only specified amendments are allowed. Closed rules, however, also protect representatives from having to decide between good politics and good tax policy.[12]

There are two different sources for collective indecisiveness in Congress on the budget. Firstly, member preferences on the budget may be irrational or inconsistent and a legislator finds no budget satisfactory. Individual legislators may find themselves with inconsistent budgetary preferences, much like the country as a whole. Secondly, due to lack of agreement and unwillingness to compromise, individual budgetary preferences may not be aggregated into a single budget policy supported by the majority. It is possible, therefore, that even if members do have individually rational preferences, there will be no one budget on which a majority can agree.[13]

Democracy complicates budgeting because it is widely held that spending money helps one electorally and imposing costs is politically harmful. Members of Congress can avoid making politically difficult decisions while they blame the president, the bureaucracy, or interest groups for being the real culprit for rising deficits. For citizens, it is difficult to assess who is responsible for large deficits. Ultimately, public opinion and the beliefs of our political leaders are the strongest forces in our budget process. Members of Congress often feel compelled to serve general interests only when a program's cost or benefits are salient or potentially salient to a substantial number of citizens, and only if coalition leaders employ procedures that encourage traceability for general effects rather than for groups or geographic effects. The extent to which our representatives anticipate citizen preferences about general costs and benefits depends on the relative size and visibility of those general effects compared with the size and visibility of group and geographic effects.[14]

Most members of Congress are forced to specialize–to focus their attention on one or a few areas of public policy and develop some measure of expertise in these fields. Since it would be impossible for an individual to know all the details about every bill on which a member of Congress must vote, one must resort to relying on other members of Congress for information. Cue taking from other members of Congress is commonplace.[15] Members of Congress tend to look toward their friends, ideologically similar members, state delegates, party leaders, the president, and members on the committee in which the bill originated for cues on how to vote. Furthermore, on a good share of budget issues, it is relatively easy for a member of Congress to figure out where he or she stands because of the ideological dimensions of the issue. One's own personal beliefs are key to explaining how a member of Congress votes; compared to the general public, those elected to Congress have relatively stable and consistent ideological beliefs. Members of Congress claim that they rarely compromise their ideological convictions in the face of opposing forces when voting on budget issues.[16] As guides to vote choice, however, ideological theories are not always reliable predictors.

Undoubtably, the influences on the congressional budget process include more than simply representatives' own beliefs. A number of "Madisonian" institutional factors are continually pressuring congressional actions on the budget, including separation of powers (which will be discussed in Chapter 4) and bicameralism. Within Congress itself, however, the most important structural entity influencing the budget process is something that is not even in the Constitution: the committee system. Given the significance of the committee system in the budget process, it is important to determine if the committee system biases Congress toward particular budgetary outcomes. That inquiry will be the focus of the remainder of this chapter.

Committees and the Congressional Budget Process

Committee assignments are best understood as a set of institutional arrangements that channel member interests into positions of legislative advantage. Committees are central to congressional decision-making because they serve the interests of both the institution and individual members. By dividing into workgroups, Congress saves time, gains expertise and encourages specialization. Committees divide labor in order to handle a large and complex workload. Members of Congress are encouraged to work diligently on their committee work because their decisions often determine policy outcomes. Committees separate issues into manageable pieces. All told, committees are a means to come to policy agreements, and they are designed to stabilize political influence over policy areas.

Committee power can be seen as having both a negative and positive character. Negative committee power is the ability to defend the status quo from others who favor change. Negative power rests on the ability of a committee to restrict the choices available to the chamber. Positive committee power is the ability of a committee to change a policy despite the fact that others oppose change. Positive power rests on the ability of a committee to circumvent the floor or to convince some members to vote for the committee position contrary to their own true political beliefs. Negative committee power is a much better description of the committee process, at least when it comes to budgeting.[17] Even though committees to a certain degree can be seen as a means of facilitating the legislative process, the committee system can also be seen as inhibiting change, especially in the House (though this dynamic may be less due to committees per se and more to the absence of some larger, integrative force like a disciplined party or strong chamber leadership). Policy-making in the United States typically has been very slow moving. The fact that the committee system can inhibit change adds another barrier to Congress' attempt to agree on significant spending cuts or revenue increases. If spending cuts are passed, there is a secondary effect on the value of current legislative commitments which dominate the manner in which Congress does its work–spending cuts would be considered a reneging on past contracts.[18]

A whole range of committees deal with taxing and spending; there is no single focal point in the budget process. There are five major players in the committee organization relevant to the budget, these being the House and Senate Budget committees, the House and Senate Appropriations committees, the House Ways and Means Committee and Senate Finance Committee, the authorization committees, and the CBO. The authorization committees set policy, the appropriation committees determine the levels and distribution of discretionary spending, and the taxation committees determine the volume of revenues and the distribution of the tax burden. All of these activities are supposed to be coordinated by the budget committees, with the help of the CBO, so that Congress can meet its policy obligations and budget deficit targets.

According to House rules, no appropriation shall be reported in any general appropriations bill for any expenditure not previously authorized by law. The Appropriations committee, however, is not expected to make such reductions as will place on-going or newly authorized programs in jeopardy.[19] The authorization requirement serves to highlight the fact that the primary responsibility of Congress is to provide services, not to make budgetary decisions. The authorization committees are organized according to governmental function. In the House, a total of 18 committees share some authorization responsibility.[20] The Budget committees, created in 1974, were supposed to help centralize the budget process. Once the budget resolutions are passed, it is the responsibility of the budget committees to try to enforce them. Though their record in challenging the spending preferences of other committees is mixed, the budget committees have made very little headway in reducing the discretion of the revenue committees of Congress.[21] All told, the committee system is not designed for efficient budgeting and hinders the coordination of the extremely complex budget process.

Members of Congress have three primary goals: 1) re-election; 2) influence within Congress; and 3) good public policy. Committees represent a means to these goals. Though most members of Congress seek all three of these goals, members also tend to prioritize them, and different committees provide different benefits to legislators.[22] The Appropriations and Ways and Means/Finance committees are populated mostly by influence-oriented members. They are forced to worry about what other members want. Thus, the other members are an environmental constraint on these members. These particular committees are especially important among the many congressional committees because of the policies they handle and the connection between these policies and the power of Congress within the American political system. House members want these two committees to be influential committees by being able to make independent policy judgments that are supported by the institution as a whole. At the same time, however, Congress wants these two committees to have a special degree of responsiveness. Because of the power and influence of these committee members, party leaders play a more active part in the recruitment and selection for these two committees than for others.[23] Taxing and spending, after all, are often considered to be the most important legislative powers in representative democracies.

The Appropriations Committees

Forty years ago the "budget process" by-and-large meant appropriations. Historically, legislative control of the budget has been accomplished through appropriations. The committees' fiscal powers have been, and remain to a lesser degree, far-reaching. The power of appropriations can be seen by the fact that the heads of the 13 appropriation subcommittees are broadly known as the "College of Cardinals." Every year Appropriations is charged with producing the 13 spending bills that keep government running. Appropriations committee members were powerful because before the rise of entitlements they were in charge of allocating largely discretionary monies. Even with the rise of entitlements, however, the Appropriations committees still have the greatest amount of money under their jurisdiction, though this now represents less than half of the total.[24] As David Obey, former House Appropriations Chair, noted, Appropriations "plays a central role in defining the party and in defining the House. It's central to the ability of the party to get its work done and to adhere to its agenda."[25]

The House Appropriations Committee is a closely knit panel that has a subculture of its own. Traditionally, it was considered less partisan and more secretive than other committees, though this is less so today, and for years its leadership was dominated by men in their 70s and 80s who tended to focus more on passing the 13 appropriations bills rather than on larger political issues.[26] The chair's power over the details of legislation, however, is limited. Most of the committee's work is done in its 13 subcommittees, which have run autonomously for years. This lack of coordination between the 13 committees has been a major source of dissatisfaction with the appropriations process.

Traditionally, the Appropriations committees have been seen as influential because they make independent judgments and carry those judgments on the House floor.[27]   During the heyday of the House Appropriations Committee, its members prided themselves on their success at getting committee recommendations accepted by the House. Being "rolled on the floor" was a mark of disgrace, showing that members were out of touch with the desires of the House as a whole. Increasingly, however, Appropriations has found itself being rolled on the floor more and more often. In 1963, the average number of amendments passed for each House appropriations bill was 2.5; now that figure is close to 10.[28]

No appropriation can be made without authorization. Authorizations are the official expressions of the interests of Congress. Even when they are inflated by wishful thinking about what future spending levels will be, authorizations are a much better claim on federal resources than are the numerous bills introduced every year. Permanent authorizations account for more than one-half of the federal budget. Many of the major programs and agencies established since after World War II, however, have temporary (annual or multi-year) authorizations. By limiting the terms of authorizations, virtually every House and Senate committee has gained some role in the formation of congressional budgetary policy.[29]

The Appropriations committees traditionally scrutinize executive budgetary actions and compare them to authorization requests. If authorization requests are much different from the president's requests, appropriations will often side toward the president's position. The Appropriation committees, however, are not expected to make reductions so severe that they would place established programs in jeopardy. For most annual authorizations the amount appropriated is more than 90 percent of the authorized level. This pattern is especially true when the authorization committees and Appropriations share similar program objectives. Authorizations and appropriations, however, will diverge when the committees do not share the same attitudes toward a program.

The Appropriations committees see themselves in the role of watchdog of the budget process. They were created in the 1860s in order to control governmental spending, a tradition that they have tried to maintain. In his 1966 work *The Power of the Purse*, Richard Fenno identified budget cutting as the foremost operational goal of the House Appropriations Committee. The Appropriations Committee would annually produce figures showing that they cut the budget, providing proof that they were the guardians of the purse. Traditionally, the appropriations process served two purposes. First, Congress should guard against waste and extravagance. Second, Congress should control executive budget actions.[30]   The Appropriations committees' decision rules call for a balance between budget reduction and program support, with priority going to budget reduction.[31]   However, where their own constituents are affected, the Appropriations committees have used their enormous leverage to secure favorable outcomes for committee members' constituents.

These contradictory policy goals of Appropriations can be seen by the divergent views toward appropriations expressed by the chairs of the House and Senate Appropriations committees during the 103rd Congress.   Robert Byrd, the chair of the Senate Appropriations Committee at the time, believed his job as chair was to get as much federal funding to his home state of West Virginia as possible. For Byrd, appropriations is a means to the pork-barrel.   David Obey, Byrd's counterpart in the House, took much more of a guardian view. Despite his liberal and party loyalist inclinations, Obey believed that spending had to be curtailed and advocated cuts for such items as NASA's costly space station. Obey, who succeeded two chairmen who had been in their 80s (William Natcher and James Whitten) whose views toward appropriations were much like Byrd's, found that he had to walk a fine line between making the kinds of changes his supporters expected from a committed liberal reformer of the younger generation on the one hand, and jarring one of Congress' most tradition-bound committees on the other.[32]

The old authorizations-appropriating dichotomy no longer works as well as it once did. The old relationship does not apply any longer because Congress has increasingly wanted to guarantee payments to individuals. The rising role and power of subcommittees due to the complexity of bills has also hurt the traditional process by decentralizing it further. The boundaries between authorizing and appropriating are difficult to distinguish. Because of the changing budgetary environment, the appropriation committees have seen themselves withdraw from their previous positions as guardians of the treasury since the mid-1970s; the traditional support for committee norms are no longer evident as committee members have increasingly sought greater self-expression.[33]   For many members of Congress, program advocacy became the main purpose of appropriations as opposed to holding down spending.

From 1921 until the early 1970s, the Appropriations committees dominated the budget process. Their power, however, was significantly curtailed in the 1970s by two forces.   First, dismayed by the Appropriations committees' conservative outlook on social issues, other committees devised means to get around them. A variety of back-door methods of financing were devised or extended. Second, the creation of the Budget committees usurped traditional power from Appropriations.[34] The appropriated entitlement has become the most important mechanism that Congress has employed to spread general-fund spending authority among its committees.[35]

As partisan conflict over budget priorities has intensified and produced policy stalemates, both appropriating and authorizing committees have lost autonomy to party leaders and the Budget committees which sought to resolve the budgetary conflicts. Authorizing committees have suffered greatly in the new age of deficit politics, as they are now limited in new legislative initiatives and have turned to focusing their energy to preserving programs they supported in the past. Reconciliation cut sharply into the traditional power of authorizing committees by forcing cuts on matters under their jurisdiction.[36] Similarly, the Appropriations committees have expressed concerns that their powers have been curtailed by reconciliation, which is under the direction of the Budget committees. From the perspective of the Appropriations committees, if the reconciliation bill passes, power is centralized in the Budget committees, further reducing their power in the budget process.

With the Budget Act of 1974, the guardian role passed from the Appropriations committees to the Budget committees. The former guardians were now seen as claimants, who had to be monitored if the budget was to remain under control.[37] The Appropriations committees have not taken lightly the fact that they are now supposed to be dictated to by the Budget committees and have fought back, trying to exert their independence from the Budget committees whenever possible. The result is that instead of creating a more coherent budget process, the Budget Act of 1974 instead made it even more complex and difficult.

The Ways and Means and Finance Committees

The Ways and Means Committee in the House and the Finance Committee in the Senate create the legislation that generates the revenue for the federal government. These two committees are extremely powerful because they control sources of revenue. In addition to being responsible for tax legislation, the committees are responsible for trade and many of the largest spending programs in the budget, including Social Security and Medicare.

From their birth until the Civil War, the House Ways and Means

Committee and the Senate Finance Committee acted not only as the tax writing committees, but they also served as appropriations and banking committees as well. After the Civil War these committees were finally stripped of their appropriations and banking functions as a means of limiting spending and curtailing the power of Ways and Means/Finance. The tax-writing committees, however, are still unique in having a key role in both the revenue and expenditure sides of the budget. Today, the tax-writing committees have more power over the budget than the budget committees. Ways and Means/Finance has control of 100 percent of federal taxes and more than half of federal spending. In other words, these committees have control of nearly three-fourths of the federal budget.[38]

Since the tax-writing committees have almost complete control of the revenue side of the budget, control a good portion of the spending, and have jurisdiction over both the deficit and the national debt, many observers of Congress conclude that they have excessive control.[39] The power of the House Ways and Means can be seen by the fact that this committee (along with Appropriations and Rules) is among the most difficult in which to get selected.

It has been argued that the strategic premises of members on the Ways and Means Committee is to try to prosecute policy partisanship while attempting to write a bill that will pass the House. When forced to choose between a bill that will pass the House and the prosecution of policy partisanship, the committee will opt for the former.[40] The Finance Committee members, on the other hand, pursue policy and constituency re-election goals in a very pluralistic environment. Committee members find that they achieve a high portion of their goals by giving sympathetic treatment to clientele groups. Their decision strategy, therefore, is to give assistance to clientele groups which appeal to them for redress from House decisions. Thus, the result is that the Senate tends to decrease revenues and/or increase spending from the desires of the House. Another strategic premise of members of Finance is to seek policy individualism–each member pursues his or her own view of good public policy in concert with whatever allies he or she can find.[41] This, however, is an extremely difficult way to design a coherent macroeconomic plan for the government's spending and taxing. Neither of the strategic premises of the Finance Committee, therefore, is particularly conducive toward balancing the budget.

When Wilbur Mills served as Ways and Means Chairman (1958-1974) the committee was lead by the strategic premises of trying to meet the strongly held policy ideals of party leaders while attempting to write bills that would pass on the floor. During the reform era that occurred while Al Ullman was chairman (1975-1980), however, Ways and Means became much more open and willing to take highly controversial bills to the House floor, even though the odds of the bills losing were significant. The leadership of Dan Rostenkowski (1981-1994), reflected a mixture of traditional and reform era elements. Even though Rostenkowski was not known to hold strong ideological views, he was considered to be instinctively loyal to the Democratic party as an institution and guarded the interests of the Ways and Means Committee. Though he was not as tolerant of dissenting views within the committee as Ullman was, Rostenkowski was willing to take politically risky stands on issues, and he was powerful enough to make or break tax issues.[42] Rostenkowski's role in getting the 1986 tax reform passed demonstrates, despite the reforms decentralizing the House and its committees, the potential power that remains in the hands of a Ways and Means Committee Chairperson.

During the Clinton presidency, Ways and Means was the battleground for some of President Clinton's most ambitious proposals after getting elected, including health care reform, overhaul of the welfare system, and the North American Free Trade Agreement. In a mark of how much one person can mean in the committee system, these proposals were hurt by the uncertain status of Rostenkowski, who was indicted for financial abuse of his office. Rostenkowski had so successfully centralized control of the committee in his own hands that the committee lost cohesion when he was forced to step aside. On the major budget, tax, trade and social legislation that went through Ways and Means in recent years, it had been Rostenkowski who assembled the deals, often single-handedly. Rostenkowski preferred to build a centrist bipartisan coalition in committee if possible. With a Democrat in the White House, the committee had become more partisan because of the burden it assumed for passing Clinton's program. The natural tendency of Ways and Means is to be overtly partisan, but Rostenkowski was able to moderate that somewhat because of his pragmatism and because of his interest in passing bills.[43] Thus, without Rostenkowski, the committee fell into partisan bickering and was unable to come to a consensus on legislation, as was demonstrated by the failed attempt at health care reform.

The Budget Committees

The balancing of congressional interests begins in the Budget committee. Although they can take a hard line and try to block legislation that does not meet the their rules, the Budget committees try to accommodate the budget process to the diverse legislative interests of other committees, especially those of Appropriations and Ways and Means/Finance. The dilemma for the Budget committees is to accommodate without giving up all meaningful enforcement. But the Budget committees are unable to prevent other committees from doing what they want to do.[44] Both Budget committees are really "adding-machine" committees that gather the demands of the spending committees and impose as much restraint on them as the current congressional mood allows.[45] Neither Budget committee has the authority to act as the sole interpreter of congressional preferences, greatly weakening their designated role as guardians of the budget process.

The Budget committees are Congress' macrobudgeters. The Budget committees have a key role in setting the budget parameters and in allocating funds to approximately 20 broad functional categories such as health, income security, and national defense. Theses committees, however, are not permitted to line-item their budget resolutions by specifying the programs to be funded; this is the jurisdiction of other committees. The macrobudgeting role is thus inherently flawed because the Budget committees have an extraordinarily broad scope, but little potential power.[46]

Congress wanted to make the Budget committees powerful, but not too powerful because the Appropriations and Ways and Means/Finance committees did not relish the idea of a rival Budget Committee. Thus, Congress neutralized the enormous scope of the Budget committees by denying them any legislative jurisdiction. Yet, these committees were to serve as guardians within congressional ranks because the budget is not a self-made or self-enforcing decision. The Budget committees were made somewhat independent in order to insure that they would have rivals in the budget process, thereby diluting their power. Thus, once the budget resolutions have been passed, the Budget committees must try to enforce them, often by challenging the spending preferences of other congressional committees. Also diluting the power of these committees' was the fact that there exists no automatic restraint upon the substantive range of amendments or the number of floor amendments which could substantially change the Budget committees proposals.[47]

Since its creation in 1974, the Senate Budget Committee has featured between 16-22 members chosen by party caucuses and serving indefinitely. The House Budget Committee, on the other hand, was structured so that five members came from the Appropriations Committee, five from Ways and Means, and one each from the Democratic and Republican leadership. The other members (originally 13, but expanded to more than 30 in recent years) on the committee were appointed through the usual House procedures. However, in the House membership is rotating–no member can serve more that six (originally four) years out of every ten. Rotation was devised to insure that committee members would not become too powerful or become too isolated in their viewpoints. Rotation weakens the committee because committee members can get away with crossing the chair on occasion. The temporary nature of the assignment also removes the main incentive for members to cooperate in establishing and preserving the reputation of the committee.

The result is that the Senate Budget Committee is more typical of Senate committees than the House Budget Committee is of House committees. The Senate Budget Committee is independent, influential, and effectively integrated into the Senate's decision-making process while the House Budget Committee is not a highly independent committee, and on its own does not represent an especially influential one. The Senate, therefore, has tended to support the budget process more than the House. The decision-making processes found in the internal workings of the committee are consistent with the current Senate. Power is not centralized with the chair. By not establishing a chair's mark, by using current policy estimates as a baseline, and by avoiding specific program detail, the Senate Budget Committee has made sure that the budget process fits the Senate and serves its members' needs.[48]

The House Budget Committee, on the other hand, is a hybrid–it is unlike any other committee. The House Budget Committee is "less independent in its actions, less autonomous than other committees, and has not attained integration in its highly conflictual environment."[49] The base of support in the House is tenuous, and it has been difficult for the committee to build and maintain a majority. The weakness of the House Budget Committee is exacerbated by the fact that it is not necessarily a desirable committee on which to be a member, at least compared to Appropriations and Ways and Means. Although the Budget Committee deals with huge sums of money, unlike the case with Appropriations it is difficult for members to point to tangible benefits secured for their district. A seat on the Budget Committee is usually not sought after to enhance reelection chances. Constituency pressures associated with the budget resolutions appear to be significantly greater in the House than the Senate.[50] In fact, some House members indicate that service on the Budget Committee is detrimental to re-election because support of budget resolutions has caused problems back in the district. This was certainly the case in 1994, when Democrats such as David Price of North Carolina, who was considered to be from a safe Democratic district, lost due in part to his opponent's criticism of Price's support for the 1994 budget resolution, which raised taxes.

The House Budget Committee has been more polarized between liberals and conservatives than the Senate Budget Committee. The ideological distance between Democrats and Republicans on the Budget Committee is much greater in the House than the Senate. The Senate Budget Committee has a tradition of being relatively bipartisan. Partisanship, however, has always been a central aspect of House Budget Committee decision-making. Unrestrained partisanship dominates. The fiscal 1995 House budget resolution, for example, which was a slightly modified version of the budget President Clinton sent to Congress, was approved by the committee 26-17 along strict party lines. In a mirror image of their final vote on the modified Clinton budget, committee Democrats unanimously voted against the Republican alternative budget, which received the votes of all the Republicans on the committee.[51]

Representativeness of the Congressional Money Committees

Are the Budget, Ways and Means/Finance and Appropriations committees representative of the rest of Congress, or do they consist of congressional outliers? It has been found that committees composed of preference outliers are rare–congressional committees do not tend to be biased subsets of their parent chambers. Accordingly, most standing committees do not have general ideology medians or means significantly different from the House.[52] On the other hand, Richard Fenno wrote in 1973 that the Ways and Means committee was consistently more partisan–across all policy areas–than was the House as a whole, and he found that the House Appropriations Committee was consistently less partisan than the chamber as a whole.[53] Since the committees that deal with budgetary issues are so powerful, any biases reflected in these committees, whether they be in terms of ideology or the types of districts they represent, would have important implications for budgeting and democratic accountability.

Table 3.1
**A Comparison of the Characteristics of Members
and Nonmembers of the Budget, Appropriations, and
Ways and Means/Finance Committees**

Budget Committees

	House		Senate	
Variable	*Members*	*Nonmembers*	*Members*	*Nonmembers*
Ideology	50.9	50.2	49.4	50.3
% Rural	24.7	24.8	29.3	32.5
% White	79.7	75.2	81.7	84.3
% College	46.6	44.8	46.5	44.9
Per Capita Income	14.9	14.4	13.9	13.6
% Vote for Clinton (1992)	43.2	43.8	41.8	41.0
% Vote for Perot (1992)	18.8	18.4	18.8	20.1
% Vote in Last Election	65.3	63.2	58.6	60.9
Years Served	8.8	10.8	10.0	11.5
Party Unity Score	86.8	88.4	86.3	85.4
Presidential Support Score	65.1	65.2	64.9	66.5

Appropriations Committees

	House		Senate	
Variable	*Members*	*Nonmembers*	*Members*	*Nonmembers*
Ideology	53.7	49.7	50.0	50.2
% Rural	27.9	24.3	30.7	32.3
% White	74.8	75.9	81.7	84.6
% College	43.8	45.1	45.0	45.2
Per Capita Income	13.9	14.5	13.6	13.7
% Vote for Clinton (1992)	45.4	43.5	42.6	40.7
% Vote for Perot (1992)	17.3	18.7	19.2	20.1
% Vote in Last Election	65.9	63.0	58.8	61.0
Years Served	14.4	10.0*	12.6	10.7
Party Unity Score	90.2	88.0	86.8	85.1
Presidential Support Score	70.0	64.4	65.4	66.5

Table 3.1 (Continued)

Ways and Means/Finance Committees

Variable	House Members	House Nonmembers	Senate Members	Senate Nonmembers
Ideology	54.8	49.8	54.2	49.1
% Rural	18.4	25.4	34.0	31.3
% White	74.7	75.8	88.2	82.7
% College	46.7	44.8	44.5	45.4
Per Capita Income	14.6	14.4	13.0	13.8
% Vote for Clinton (1992)	46.8	43.5	41.1	41.2
% Vote for Perot (1992)	17.2	18.6	21.3	19.5
% Vote in Last Election	66.8	63.1	65.3	59.1
Years Served	12.6	10.2	13.9	10.6
Party Unity Score	89.8	88.1	86.2	85.4
Presidential Support Score	68.2	64.9	69.5	65.4

*p < .05

Each figure represents the mean total of respective committee members in the House and Senate.

Definition of Variables: Ideology = member's ideological score, as measured by the *National Journal* (with 0 = most conservative and 100 = most liberal); % Rural = percentage of member's district (for House)/state (for Senate) that is rural according to the U.S. census (1990); % White = percentage of member's district/state that is listed as white according to the U.S. census (1990); % College = percentage of the district/state with 2 or more years of college; Per Capita Income = per capita income of member's district/state, in thousands; % Vote for Clinton (1992) = percentage of member's district/state that voted for Bill Clinton in 1992; % Vote for Perot (1992) = percentage of member's district/state that voted for Ross Perot in 1992; % Vote in Last Election = percentage of the vote the member received in his/her most recent general election; Years Served = years that the legislator has served in the House or Senate; Party Unity Score = percentage of the time the member voted with a majority of his/her party against a majority of the other party, as compiled by *Congressional Quarterly*; Presidential Support Score = percentage of the time that the member supported the Clinton administration's position on a bill during the 103rd Congress (1993-1994), as compiled by *Congressional Quarterly*.

Table 3.1 displays the means for members and nonmembers of the House and Senate money committees during the 103rd Congress (1993-1994) for eight different variables. These findings reveal that there is remarkably little difference between committee members and nonmembers. The only statistically significant ($p < .05$) explanatory variable was the number of years members on the House Appropriations Committee had served in the House: Appropriations Committee members generally had more House seniority than nonmembers. This is probably the result of the fact that few freshmen and sophomores get on this prestigious committee–most members must wait a number of terms to get on Appropriations.[54]

For the other House committees, the Ways and Means Committee and the Budget Committee, no variables were statistically significant. Thus, Fenno's claim that the Ways and Means Committee was more partisan than the whole House did not appear to hold true during the 103rd Congress. The House Budget Committee, which was created after Fenno's 1973 analysis of the committee system, appears to be an unbiased subset of the total body–none of the variables were statistically significant.

For all three committees in the Senate there were no statistically significant variables. This finding suggests that the Senate committees are apparently unbiased subsets of the entire Senate. This is consistent with the literature on Senate committees. The major reason this should be expected is that the partisan balance on these Senate committees is more equitable than it is in the House, and a greater percentage of Senators are on each committee than in the House, which will tend to make Senate committees, by their very nature, more representative of the entire body.[55]

Conclusion

Structurally, Congress, is not designed in a manner conducive toward budgeting. Though many of the seemingly problematic features of the congressional budget process were not designed by the Founding Fathers, the manner in which the political institutions of the United States were designed may be partly to blame for the difficulty Congress has in budgeting. In their desire to limit the "tyranny of the majority," the Founding Fathers created a legislative body that was destined to be inefficient. Yet, while Congress is not structured in a manner that makes it easy to pass the complex legislation that the budget has become as we move toward the 21st century, the structure of Congress does not make it impossible to enact a sensible budget either.

The complexity of the congressional budget process is magnified by the nature of the committee system. The committee system is at the heart of the American legislative process. To understand the actions that Congress takes, one has to understand the dynamics of congressional committees. There are three important committees which have the primary responsibility for producing the nation's budget: Appropriations, Ways and Means/Finance, and Budget. Each of these "money" committees sees their role in the budget process somewhat differently and, to a large degree, these committees have contradictory policy goals. The money committees, therefore, are often in conflict when it comes to budgeting.

The conflict between these committees appears to be the result of the committees' function in the budget process rather than a result of the varied membership of these committees. An analysis of the representativeness of the congressional money committees shows that the Budget, Appropriations, and Ways and Means/Finance committees are not in any way an "outlier" from other committees. That is, the membership of the money committees tends to be consistent with the membership of other congressional committees. This finding is important for the concept of democratic accountability of the budget process. Budgetary outcomes appear to be the result of the normal dynamics of the committee system. The budget does not appear to be manipulated by members unrepresentative of the body as a whole. Though the committee system may have many faults and may not be the best way to budget, budgetary outcomes are, for better or worse, a natural part of this process.

Endnotes

1. Donald F. Kettl, *Deficit Politics* (New York: Longman, 2003), p. 1.

2. Robert Lee and Ronald Johnson, *Public Budgeting Systems*, 5th ed. (Brunswick, OH: King's Court Press, 1994), p. 6.

3. Joseph White and Aaron Wildavsky, *The Deficit and the Public Interest* (Berkeley: University of California Press, 1989), p. 1.

4. Ibid., p. 6.

5. Kettl (2003), p. 1.

6. Allen Schick, *The Capacity to Budget* (Washington: The Urban Institute, 1990), pp. 1-3.

7. V.O. Key, "The Lack of Budgetary Theory," *American Political Science Review* 34 (1940): 1137-1140.

8. Verne Lewis, "Toward a Theory of Budgeting," *Public Administration Review* 12 (1952): 43-54.

9. Bryan D. Jones, Tracy Sulkin, and Heather A. Larsen, "Policy Punctuations in American Political Institutions," *American Political Science Review* 97 (2003): 151-169.

10. Richard Rose, "Maximizing Tax Revenue While Minimizing Political Costs," *Journal of Public Policy* 5 (1986): 289-320.

11. Ibid., p. 312.

12. David Rosenbaum, "I'll Sleep on the Idea, but Must I Vote On It?" *The New York Times*, (February 2, 1995), p. A10.

13. John B. Gilmour, *Reconcilabe Differences?* (Berkeley: University of California Press, 1990), pp. 226-229.

14. R. Douglas Arnold, *The Logic of Congressional Action* (New Haven: Yale University Press, 1990), p. 142.

15. Donald Mathews and James Stimson, *Yeas and Neas* (New York: John Wiley and Sons, 1975), chapter 3.

16. Ibid.

17. Steven Smith and Christopher Deering, *Committees in Congress* (Washington: CQ Press, 1990), p. 9.

18. Mark Crain, "Legislatures and the Durability of Deficits," *Deficits*, James Buchanan, Charles Rowley, and Robert Tollison eds. (New York: Basil Blackwell), pp. 287-288.

19. Richard F. Fenno, *The Power of the Purse* (Boston: Little, Brown and Company, 1966), p. 15.

20. Daniel Franklin, *Making Ends Meet* (Washington, D.C.: Congressional Quarterly, 1993), pp. 40-42.

21. Dennis Ippolito, *Congressional Spending* (Ithacca: Cornell University Press, 1981), pp. 96-98.

22. Richard Fenno, *Congressmen in Committees* (Boston: Little, Brown and Company, 1973).

23. Ibid., pp. 13-18.

24. Lance Leloup,   *Budgetary Politics* (King's Court Press: Brunswick, OH, 1977), p. 123.

25. Janet Hook, "Race for Appropriations Chair Pits Activism vs. Stability," *Congressional Quarterly* (March 19, 1994), pp. 647-650.

26. Janet Hook and George Hager, "Appropriations Under Obey Will Have a Harder Edge," *Congressional Quarterly* (March 26, 1994), pp. 713-714.

27. Fenno (1973), pp. 193-202.

28. Aaron Wildavsky and Naomi Caiden, *The New Politics of the Budgetary Process*, 4th ed. (New York: Longman, 2001).

29. Allen Schick, *Congress and Money* (Washington: AEI, 1980), pp. 171-173.

30. Fenno (1966).

31. Fenno (1973), p. 193.

32. George Hager, "In an Unlikely Role for a Partisan...Obey Is Making his Mark," *Congressional Quarterly* (May 14, 1994), pp. 1178-1179.

33. Wildavsky and Caiden (2001), pp. 19-20.

34. Howard Shuman, *Politics and the Budget* (Englewood Cliffs: Prentice Hall, 1988), p. 64.

35. Ibid., p. 24.

36. Smith and Deering (1990), pp. 211-212.

37. Naomi Caiden, "The Politics of Subtraction," *Making Economic Policy in Congress*, Allen Schick ed. (Washington: AEI, 1983), p. 111.

38. Shuman (1988), pp. 120-128.

39. Lance Leloup, *The Fiscal Congress* (Westport, CT: Greenwood Press, 1980), pp. 126-127.

40. Fenno (1973), pp. 47-57 and p. 202.

41. Ibid., pp. 156-160.

42. Randall Strahan, "Dan Rostenkowski: A Study in Congressional Power," *Congress Reconsidered*, 5th ed., Lawrence Dodd and Bruce Oppenheimer eds., pp. 189-210 (Washington: CQ Press, 1993).

43. David Cloud, "Ways and Means in Turmoil Over Chairmans' Fate," *Congressional Quarterly* (May 28, 1994), p. 1369.

44. Schick (1980), pp. 369-370.

45. Ippolito (1981), chapter 4.

46. John Cogan, Timothy Muris and Allen Schick, *The Budget Puzzle* (Stanford: Stanford University Press, 1994), pp. 12-13.

47. Schick (1980), chapter 4.

48. Ippolito (1981), pp. 84-85.

49. Leloup (1980), p. 81.

50. Ibid., p. 103.

51. George Hager, "House Budget Panel Leaves Clinton Plan Largely Intact," *Congressional Quarterly* (March 5, 1994), pp. 525-526.

52. Keith Krehbiel, "Are Committees Composed of Preference Outliers?" *American Political Science Review* 84 (1990): 149-164, and Richard Hall and Bernard Grofman, "The Committee Assignment Process and the Conditional Nature of Committee Bias," *American Political Science Review* 84 (1990): 1149-1166.

53. Fenno (1973), p. 202.

54. Patrick Fisher, "Committees and the Budget Process: How Representative are Congressional Budgeting Committees?" *Southeastern Political Review* 25 (1997): 769-780.

55. Ibid.

Chapter 4

Separation of Powers and the
Budget Process

An important element in the budget process is the degree to which it is dominated by the executive or legislative branch. The Constitution split budgetary power between the president and Congress. At various times, however, one branch of government has tended to have the upper hand in the budget process. From the earliest days of American government, budget decisions have been treated as a struggle for power between the executive and legislative branches. Roots of the legislative budget go back to colonial times; there were extraordinary efforts of colonial legislators to control executives by limiting their expenditures. Anti-monarchy beliefs led to anti-executive tendencies when it came to the power of budgeting and taxing.[1] The experience of the United States, however, has tended to indicate that budgeting requires the strong central force of an executive.

The Rise of Presidential Budgetary Power
The modern presidency began with the Budget and Accounting Act of 1921, in which Congress delegated its traditional powers over compiling the preliminary draft of the budget to the president. The law required the president to develop and submit a budget to Congress and

established the Bureau of the Budget (later the Office of Management and Budget). The expansion of the role of government during the Progressive Era and World War I greatly strained the traditional congressional budget process. Before 1921, if agencies wanted money, they went directly to Congress–the president had little budgetary power. Congress, unable to cope to the new budgetary environment and realizing that more centralization was needed in the budget process, was forced to forfeit some of its power of the purse to the president in 1921. Congress gave the president more power in the budget process because it found itself unable to cope with the rising demands of government and the dogma of public administration in the Progressive Era placed great faith in a nonpolitical executive having responsibility for the budget. The result is that the president has become the dominant force in developing budget policies and procedures. The president's budget sets the priorities and goals for the country. This has not, however, made the budget process any less complicated, fairer, or more efficient. To some, the Budget Act of 1921 is the heart of the budget problem. The current budget process is too complex and overwhelmingly cumbersome. The budget has become so consuming that there is little time for Congress to work on other matters. The executive budget is far different than it was 50 years ago. Today, most of the current budget is locked in by previous decisions. The executive budget may no longer provide the advantages that its sponsors assumed in 1921 and thus may have become a burden to the budget process.[2]

Congress has looked toward the president to lead the process of forming the national budget ever since the Budget Act of 1921 made the president responsible for submitting a budget proposal to Congress. Unfortunately, presidents have generally not shown much interest in budgeting. It has been difficult to get the president to acknowledge budgetary problems and seek solutions. For the most part, presidents focus on other priorities. Even a president who was actively involved in the budgetary process, however, would still be constrained by political considerations. Furthermore, a president must pay attention to public opinion if he is to be successful. Many decisions a president could try to implement to improve the budget, such as reducing the deficit, would be wildly unpopular and therefore damage the president's standing with the public. Most recent presidents have shown little willingness to expend their own popularity making difficult decisions on the budget, sending budgets to Congress that were "dead on arrival," making the president's budget proposal little more than a ritual.

After the 1921 Budget Act was enacted, the president's control over the budget process continued to expand. As government grew in size, it was the White House and its budget office that kept pace, though Congress continued to exercise the power of the purse through appropriations. Congress saw its budgetary power gradually taken over by the president until it finally rebelled in 1974 due to the perceived excesses of President Nixon's budgetary policies. The basic provisions of the 1921 Budget Act, therefore, remained intact until the process finally broke down during the Nixon administration. Congress reacted by overhauling the budget process with the Congressional Budget and Impoundment Control Act of 1974, in which Congress tried to exert more control over the budget process. The Budget Act of 1974 was born out of the budgetary conflicts between Congress and the presidency arising in the period 1966-1973–a period which has been referred to as the "Seven-Year Budget War."[3]

Impoundments were a key part of the battle. Impoundments occur when the president refuses to allow executive branch agencies to spend money that has be allocated by Congress. In impoundment battles, the president had the advantage versus Congress. Although impoundments were not recognized by law, inaction meant that the president's priorities would triumph. The longer the dispute dragged on, the greater the loss of congressional control over the purse.[4] The 1974 law strengthened Congress institutionally by limiting impoundments, and by granting Congress greater responsibility over the budget.

To a large degree, budget reform in 1974 was a reaction to the criticism by the White House that Congress was not capable of budgeting responsibly. At the same time, Congress felt that it must begin to act financially responsible if it did not want to lose ultimate authority to the president. The Budget Act of 1974 may have insulated the budget from presidential influence, but by doing so it forced Congress to face greater budgetary responsibilities. Since 1974, Congress has found budgeting to be increasingly difficult. Congress found that fiscal policy determination can be frustrating in the extreme, and budget priorities are difficult to agree upon and–once determined–often resistant to change despite changes in the fiscal condition of the nation. The enormous deficits of the 1980s and the inability of Congress to come to agreement with President Bush in 1990 lead to the enactment of the Budget Enforcement Act of 1990, in which Congress once again abdicated some budgetary power to the president.

Conflict between Congress and the President

Congress and the presidency are designed not to get along. The Founding Fathers, in order to insure that one branch of the government did not become too powerful, designed a system of government where the legislative and executive branches would be rivals. Since Congress is a decentralized body of 535 members, Congress often appears weak compared to the executive branch, which is more likely to speak with one voice. Since the New Deal era, the presidency has gradually taken on increasing budgetary power while Congress has often seemed unable to gain control over its own diverse institutional self-interests. Today, there seems to be little doubt that the executive branch has become a more powerful player in the budget process than Congress, despite the intentions of the Founding Fathers. This does not mean that Congress has become irrelevant, however–far from it. In order for presidential legislative proposals to become law, after all, they must be passed by Congress. Congress may be held in low esteem by the public, the president, and even by many of its own members,, but the "power of the purse" granted to it by the Constitution still makes it a major player in the budget process.

The president and Congress have different bases of support since the president is elected from a national constituency while members of Congress are selected from individual states or districts. The two branches also have different calendars for running for reelection. The president feels pressured for time, while members of Congress are in less of hurry because they plan to be around longer. In terms of producing a coherent budget, the constitutionally-derived conflict between the two branches is magnified. Both sides want to please their own constituents and do not want to give in to the interests of the other branch. This is especially the case when one party controls Congress and the other the White House, which has been the rule rather than the exception since the Eisenhower presidency. The result has been a budgeting quagmire.

The office of President is unique because he is elected indirectly by the entire citizenry. He is the national chief executive officer and commander-in-chief of the armed forces. The president is also the chief legislator, with a vote worth 2/3 of each house of Congress due to his ability to veto legislation. The nature of the job, therefore, combined with the tremendous rise in scope of the federal government, has made the president the major player in the budget process in the twentieth century. The president's budget proposal is a very influential factor in congressional budgeting. The power of the presidency in the budget process can be seen by the fact that even when Congress refuses to endorse presidential spending cuts (as was often the case during the Reagan-Bush years), the president's budget proposals constrain authorizing legislation and lead to lower appropriations than might be expected. Even though the president's proposed budget is not necessarily an accurate guide to congressional action, it has been transformed into an opening bargaining maneuver.[5]   Especially in periods of divided government, the White House has approached the budget as a piece of legislation sent to Congress in the expectation that substantial changes would be made. The president must face the risk that his budget proposal will be changed drastically by the Appropriations committees.[6] Thus the White House, despite its pretensions, does not completely control budget policy.

Politics is unquestionably the core of budgeting and budgetary politics inevitably involves disputes over political power.[7] If budgetary decisions are important, so too is the decision about who decides and the power to decide shapes the nature of the decision.[8] Thus, an important element in the budget process is the degree to which it is dominated by the executive or legislative branch. In the model of executive dominance, the chief executive is responsible for formulating the budget proposal, which reflects priorities and the policy agenda; the legislature acts essentially as a rubber-stamp body. In the legislative dominated budget process, the bureau chiefs write up their requests for spending with the assistance of legislators who want some particular expenditures. The requests are not scrutinized by the chief executive, but are handed directly to the legislature for review and approval, with little role for the chief executive.[9]

The fact that the president has the ability to command more public attention than Congress no doubt hinders congressional influence in the budget process. Yet, despite the increased budgetary power of the presidency, Congress still has an important role protecting the public's interest. The public, judging from opinion polls, trusts Congress no more than the president. Congress, however, still sees itself as playing a protective role vis-a-vis the public's interest. Their major weapon is the "power of the purse"–Congress must pass all budget decisions. The power of the purse is the heart of legislative authority and an essential check on the executive branch. On the impoundment side of the budget, Congress tends to treat its decisions on spending as sacred; the congressional attitude is defensive on this topic. On the other hand, where supplemental appropriations are at issue, Congress accepts and even encourages limits on its abilities to say no. By refusing to set strict standards for consideration of supplemental appropriations, Congress allows the executive branch to gain routine approval for even discretionary supplemental requests, doing little to enhance its fiscal austerity.[10]

From the end of World War II until 1999, Congress never changed the president's aggregate budget request by more than 2 percent.[11] Table 4.1 is a comparison of the president's budget proposals and the final budget resolution passed by Congress from 1990-2000. Though the mix of spending (defense or social programs, etc.) may change in ways not revealed by the aggregates, the aggregate differences tend to be relatively small, with the exception of fiscal years 1999-2000. Congress tended to increase revenue and outlay totals for Republican-proposed budgets (1990-1993), but during the Clinton years decreased proposed revenue and outlay totals. Congress may be reacting against the perceived excesses of presidential proposals, with Republicans being seen as too anti-spending and anti-taxing and Democrats as too pro-spending and pro-taxing. But for both Democratic and Republican presidents (again with the exceptions of 1999-2000) the overall changes tend to be relatively minor.

The abilities of presidents vis-a-vis Congress can be seen in the finding that presidential campaigning has a significant effect on the vote choice. In other words, when presidents campaign, congressional candidates of their party do better. This makes many members of Congress somewhat beholden to the president for political help. Among the reasons for this is that presidential campaigning stimulates turnout.[12] That public prestige is an important source of presidential influence in Congress can also be seen in the finding that public opinion is an important source of presidential influence in Congress. This may be a result of the fact that the president is chosen by the electorate of the entire nation, while members of Congress are chosen only from individual districts. This can give the president a legitimate claim that he represents the entire country, a claim that is harder to refute when the president is popular. Also, if a president is popular and his agenda is not passed, members of Congress may be held accountable. There is a sense of "common fate" among members of Congress–the public holds government, including both the executive and legislative branches, responsible for any perceived policy failures.[13]

Congress is responsible for enacting appropriation legislation. The impetus and starting point for appropriation legislation, however,

Table 4.1
Presidential Budget Proposals and Actual Budget Enactments

Year		President's Budget	Budget Resolution	Difference
1990				
	Revenues	1,059.3	1,065.5	6.2
	Outlays	1,151.8	1,165.3	13.5
1991				
	Revenues	1,170.2	1,172.9	2.7
	Outlays	1,233.3	1,236.9	3.6
1992				
	Revenues	1,172.2	1,169.2	-3.0
	Outlays	1,442.2	1,448.0	5.8
1993				
	Revenues	1,171.2	1,173.0	1.8
	Outlays	1,503.0	1,500.0	-3.0
1994				
	Revenues	1,242.1	1,241.8	-0.3
	Outlays	1,500.6	1,495.6	-5.0
1995				
	Revenues	1,353.8	1,338.2	-15.6
	Outlays	1,518.9	1,513.6	-5.3
1996				
	Revenues	1,415.5	1,417.2	1.7
	Outlays	1,612.1	1,587.5	-24.6
1997				
	Revenues	1,495.2	1,469.0	-26.2
	Outlays	1,612.1	1,560.3	-51.8
1998				
	Revenues	1,566.8	1,602.0	35.2
	Outlays	1,687.5	1,652.6	-34.9
1999				
	Revenues	1,742.7	1,318.0	-424.7
	Outlays	1,733.2	1,401.1	-332.1
2000				
	Revenues	1,833.0	1,408.1	-424.9
	Outlays	1,765.7	1,408.1	-357.6

Totals are in billions of $.
Source: *Vital Statistics on Congress 2001-2002*, Norman Ornstein, Thomas Mann and Michael Malbin eds. (Washington: CQ Press, 2002), pp. 158-160.

now resides in the Executive Office of the President, specifically the Office of Management and Budget (OMB). The OMB not only controls most agency requests for funding and oversees the expenditures of appropriated funds, but it also is empowered to oversee and reject agency regulations for being cost-ineffective. Traditionally, it is the agencies, not the OMB, that have had the major responsibility for defending their budget requests before Congress. Some organizational units, such as the FBI in the 1950s and 1960s, were able to secure extensive support within Congress, thus providing them with some autonomy vis-a-vis their departments and OMB. Beginning in the 1980s, OMB gained greater responsibility for explaining and defending the president's budget before Congress; this role was largely negative because its main task was to explain how and why reductions should be made in agencies' budgets. The OMB now has more than 500 permanent employees and an annual budget of about $50 million. The budget director has become a prime actor in the budget process.[14]

For most of its history, Congress was the major player in the development of the national budget. Congress, however, gradually lost parts of its power of the purse to the executive branch until by the 1970s Congress was dependent on presidential recommendations, OMB data, and agency justifications. In order to gain a greater say in the budget process, the Congressional Budget Office (CBO) was created in 1974 to provide Congress with analyses and estimates of the budget independent of those provided by the executive branch, particularly the OMB. A major reason Congress created the CBO was that it felt, justifiably, that the OMB was politically biased in its estimates of the administration's budgetary proposals. The CBO prides itself on its neutral analyses. It serves as an important institutional resource in budget battles for it has consistently been more accurate in its economic and budget projections than the OMB. Since the mid-1980s, members of Congress have viewed the OMB as an explicitly political arm of the president in budget politics whose analysis could not be trusted.[15]

Presidents have often sent Congress budgets that relied on optimistic economic forecasts to make the numbers add up in a way to suit the president's interests. The fact that the OMB's figures have lost credibility can be seen by the fact that President Clinton has used the CBO numbers to shield the administration from attacks on its economic forecasting.[16] Clinton, in fact, became upset with the OMB under the Bush administration for showing a deficit in January 1993, after Bush lost the election, much worse than what the OMB forecast in the summer of

1992, in the middle of the presidential campaign.[17] The creation of the
CBO marked a major shift in the congressional budget process. Fifty
years ago it was sufficient to examine the Appropriations committees to
see how Congress exercised the power of the purse. This is no longer so
today.[18]

The President's Role in the Budget Process:
The Example of the 1993 Budget Reconciliation Bill

Bill Clinton, unlike most other recent presidents, demonstrated
that he would immerse himself in the details of the budget. Despite the
fact that it was not an issue that he emphasized while running for the
presidency in 1992, Clinton demonstrated a willingness early in his
presidency to reduce the deficit. It was widely held that if Clinton was to
get a handle on the deficit as he promised, he must do so in the first year
of his presidency, when his political capital was at its peak.[19]

One month into his presidency, Clinton proposed a budget that
included spending cuts, but which relied overwhelmingly on tax increases
to bring the deficit downward. At the same time, Clinton proposed to
quickly boost short-term job creation by pumping billions of dollars into
new spending programs. Clinton's deficit-cutting plan was the largest in
history, proposing to save nearly $500 billion over four years. Of that
amount, roughly two-thirds would go to reduce the deficit, while another
third would be used to pay for increased job creation and long-term
investment spending, making net deficit reduction at the end of the four
years of the plan about $325 billion.[20]

The deficit-reduction package proposed a cut of $493 billion
over four years, $247 of it coming from spending cuts and $246 billion
from tax increases, almost exactly a 1-to-1 ratio. The ratio of tax
increases to spending cuts quickly emerged as the major conflict point in
congressional reaction to the plan. Republicans and conservative
Democrats were upset that the ratio of cuts to taxes was much less than
the 2-to-1 ratio that Panetta had advocated during his confirmation
hearings. Though the deficit-reduction plan made notable spending cuts,
its heavy reliance on tax increases displays the difficulties the Clinton
economic team had coming up with acceptable spending cuts.

Clinton's call for a tax increase was a direct repudiation of the
economic philosophies of his two Republican predecessors. By aiming
the taxes primarily at corporations and the well-off, Clinton suggested that
the programs of Ronald Reagan and George Bush, which were designed

to stimulate economic growth through tax cuts, came at the price of high deficits.   Clinton believed that he could convince the American public–and a majority in Congress–that the large budget deficits of the 1980s held negative consequences in the long run.   Clinton proposed to raise most of the new revenue with an array of higher taxes on upper-income Americans and corporations, including $126.3 billion over six years mainly through a new top income tax bracket of 36 percent and a surtax on income over $250,000. Overall, more than half of the new taxes were projected to fall on families making more than $200,000 a year.[21] Table 4.2 shows the distribution of tax burden by income group.

President Clinton's proposed budget faced its biggest obstacle in Congress with the vote on the budget reconciliation bill. The budget resolution only locked in the broad deficit-reduction numbers, but left virtually all of the specifics to the reconciliation process, which was designed to reconcile tax and spending policy with deficit-reduction goals outlined in the budget resolution. The measure was the heart of Clinton's plan to reshape the nation's economic policy.

In the end, Clinton's economic plan emerged victorious, though just barely. The Omnibus Budget Reconciliation Act was approved in August 1993 without a single vote to spare in either chamber: it passed 218-217 in the House and 51-50 in the Senate (with Vice-President Al Gore making the tie-breaking vote). The measure passed without any Republican votes, the first time in postwar congressional history and possibly the first time ever that the majority party has passed major legislation with absolutely no support from the opposition.[22]

With the Republicans unwilling to compromise and unable to drive the process themselves, the struggle to get the anti-deficit package through Congress was exclusively one of rounding up enough Democrats. This was the case even though the proposal had something to offend almost every Democrat; conservatives were uncomfortable with the entire range of tax increases, and liberals were uncomfortable with some of the $87 billion in cuts over five years in entitlement spending programs such as Medicare and Medicaid as well as the $102 billion in cuts over five years in appropriated spending.[23] Liberals and the Congressional Black Caucus, however, endorsed the bill early on, making moderates and conservatives the critical swing votes.

Overall, the Clinton economic plan was expected to shrink, but not eliminate the deficit. Annual deficits under the law were expected to be around $200 billion and since nearly $500 billion in deficits was to be eliminated over five years, the national debt was expected to rise by

Table 4.2
Effect of Clinton's Tax Measures Would Have on Income Groups

	Tax Burden (1993)		Clinton Proposals		Change	
Family Income Group	Total Paid By Group	As % of Pretax Income	Total Paid By Group	As % of Pretax Income	Total Paid By Group	As % of Pretax Income
$0-10,000	$6.7	7.8	$6.5	7.6	-.2	-.2
10-20,000	26.9	9.8	26.9	9.8	0	0
20-30,000	55.7	14.0	56.0	14.1	.4	.1
30-50,000	152.1	17.3	156.5	17.8	4.4	.5
50-75,000	203.1	19.0	210.7	19.7	7.6	.7
75-100,000	174.3	20.4	180.2	21.1	5.9	.7
100-200,000	242.6	21.2	250.6	21.8	8.0	.7
200,000+	247.5	20.9	281.8	23.8	34.3	2.9

Tax Amounts are in billions.
Source: *Congressional Quarterly Weekly* (February 20, 1993), p. 364 and Treasury Dept.

"only" $1.1 trillion.[24] The plan not only marked a major step away from the low-tax and high-deficit policies of his Republican predecessors, but also from the spending-oriented policies of Democratic Congresses. By embracing the plan, if only barely, congressional Democrats gambled on their political futures, betting that deficit reduction would improve the economy in the long-run and improve their reelection prospects.

Congressional Support of the 1993 Budget Reconciliation Bill

The president has been viewed as having relatively little influence to wield over Congress.[25] Yet, when it comes to budgeting, it is clear that the president's position on budgetary priorities greatly affects congressional actions on the budget. At the same time, presidential policy success depends in part upon contextual factors that are beyond his control.[26] As a result, a president needs to devote a great deal of attention to congressional relations in order to get a budget through Congress.

This section will analyze who supported the Clinton-supported

1993 Budget Reconciliation Bill. Tables 4.3 and 4.4 compare representatives who supported the 1993 Budget with those who voted against it. The variables analyzed in Tables 4.3 and 4.4 include demographic and political characteristics of their districts as discussed in Chapter 1. Both tables demonstrate just how vast the differences were between those who supported the tax increases of the 1993 Budget Reconciliation Bill and those who opposed them.

The partisan and ideological nature of the debate surrounding the bill, as well as the fact that no Republicans voted in support of the bill, indicate that party and ideology were strongly correlated with the vote for the budget proposals. This is consistent with the finding that members of the president's party are much more open to his influence than are members of the opposing party.[27] Similarly, it has been established that members of the president's party in Congress consistently gave him strong support compared to members in the opposing party. The shared party affiliation of the president and some members of Congress serves as a source of influence for him. The president's party affiliation seems to be a source of influence in Congress, although a limited one. In domestic matters, party affiliation plays its greatest role when the president's policies are contrary to the normal stances of his party and when constituency pressures are lax enough to allow members of the president's party in Congress to respond to the pull of a member of their party in the White House.[28] To measure the importance of ideology in the vote on the 1993 Budget Reconciliation Bill, a member's floor vote history was analyzed to study the degree by which the vote on the 1993 Budget Reconciliation Bill was consistent with other votes the member made during the 103rd Congress. The ideology variable is the representative's ideological score according to the *National Journal* (with 0 being most conservative and 100 most liberal) and was chosen as a means of determining how ideological the division over the Clinton budget was.

Three district demographic characteristics (urbanization, racial composition, and per capita income) were chosen as factors to determine if district demographic characteristics offered any predictive value of the actions of Representatives and Senators on budgetary issues; previous studies have found that constituency factors predict a good share of the variation in policy positions.[29] To measure a district/state's political leanings, presidential vote in the 1992 (a rough, tough imperfect, indicator of the district's political leanings) were correlated with congressional budgetary actions. It would be expected that those districts that gave Clinton a higher percentage of the vote would more likely elect

Table 4.3
A Comparison of Legislator Characteristics for those
Who Supported and Opposed the 1993 Budget Reconciliation Bill

Vote on 1993 Budget

	House		Senate	
	For	*Against*	*For*	*Against*
Ideology	73.64	26.91***	72.84	27.42***
% Rural	21.70	27.96**	30.16	33.52
% White	68.40	83.08***	82.84	84.68
% College	43.30	46.62**	44.56	45.84
Per Capita Income	13.83	15.04**	13.98	13.30
% Vote for Clinton (1992)	51.00	36.48***	43.30	39.10***
% Vote for Perot (1992)	16.77	20.19***	18.86	20.86
% Vote in Last Election	64.43	62.37	59.82	60.90
Years Served	10.50	9.62	10.78	11.66
Party Unity Score	91.78	84.77***	86.74	84.42
Presidential Support Score	80.49	49.84***	89.72	42.64***

$*p < .05; **p < .01; ***p < .001$

Each figure represents the mean total of those who voted for and against the 1993 Budget Reconciliation Bill in the House and Senate respectively.

Definition of Variables: Ideology = member's ideological score, as measured by the *National Journal* (with 0 = most conservative and 100 = most liberal); % Rural = percentage of member's district (for House)/state (for Senate) that is rural according to the U.S. census (1990); % White = percentage of member's district/state that is listed as white according to the U.S. census (1990); % College = percentage of the district/state with two or more years of college; Per Capita Income = per capita income of member's district/state, in thousands; % Vote for Clinton (1992) = percentage of member's district/state that voted for Bill Clinton in 1992; % Vote for Perot (1992) = percentage of member's district/state that voted for Ross Perot in 1992; % Vote in Last Election = percentage of the vote the member received in his/her most recent general election; Years Served = years that the legislator has served in the House or Senate; Party Unity Score = percentage of the time the member voted with a majority of his/her party against a majority of the other party, as compiled by *Congressional Quarterly*; Presidential Support Score = percentage of the time that the member supported the Clinton administration's position on a bill during the 103rd Congress (1993-1994), as compiled by *Congressional Quarterly*.

representatives who would support the Clinton budget. Districts that gave Ross Perot a higher percentage of the 1992 presidential vote, on the other hand, may be the home of representatives who tended to dislike the Clinton proposal because it did not cut spending enough, a criticism that Perot made after Clinton proposed his 1993 budget blueprint.   It is possible, however, that those coming from a district with a higher Perot vote may have tended to support the proposal because it reduced the deficit–as a candidate Perot advocated both massive spending cuts and tax increases to reduce the deficit.

Finally, four factors representing characteristics of individual members were chosen as possible determinants of budgetary action. The percentage of the vote that the representative received in their last general election was chosen to determine if previous electoral success meant that one would be more likely to support a potentially unpopular tax-raising measure.[30] The number of years the representative served in the House or Senate is another variable analyzed. Since those with more seniority tend to come from politically "safer" districts and have more of a stake in appeasing the political leadership of the party, it may be that those with more years in their respective bodies are more likely to follow the lead of their party.[31]   Party unity scores–the percentage of the time the representative voted for a majority of their party against a majority of the other party–were chosen as a variable with the belief that those who tended to support their party more often in general were also the most likely to support the position of their party on the Clinton budget. Finally, presidential support was chosen as a variable in order to determine if the vote on the Clinton budget was typical in terms of support within the Democratic and Republican parties.

Table 4.3 shows means tests for ten factors for those who supported and opposed the 1993 Budget. This analysis displays the vast differences between those representatives, and the districts they represent, who supported the 1993 Budget Reconciliation Bill and those who opposed it.

The strength of these predictors can be seen by the fact that all of the t-ratios in Table 4.3 were statistically significant for the House with the exceptions of the vote in the last election and years served variables. For the Senate, the variables based on district characteristics proved to be poor predictors. But ideology, Clinton vote, and presidential support score variables were statistically significant. Overall, therefore, the partisan leanings of a senator's state and the partisan and ideological attributes of a senator were the best predictors of the vote on Clinton's budget

Table 4.4
A Comparison of Legislator Characteristics for Democrats
Who Supported and Opposed the 1993 Budget Reconciliation Bill

Vote on 1993 Budget

| | House | | Senate | |
	For	Against	For	Against
Ideology	73.63	49.73**	72.84	52.33**
% Rural	21.78	32.10**	30.16	27.33
% White	68.57	79.00**	82.84	76.17
% College	43.40	40.98	44.56	42.00
Per Capita Income	13.85	12.32**	13.98	13.67
% Vote for Clinton (1992)	51.01	38.98**	43.30	40.67
% Vote for Perot (1992)	16.77	19.20*	18.86	16.83
% Vote in Last Election	64.27	63.27	59.82	70.83*
Years Served	10.40	7.66**	10.78	12.50
Party Unity Score	91.76	73.56**	86.74	75.83*
Presidential Support Score	80.49	72.17**	89.72	80.83**

$*p < .05; **p < .01$

Each figure represents the mean total of those Democrats who voted for and against the 1993 Budget Reconciliation Bill in the House and Senate respectively. Definition of Variables: Ideology = member's ideological score, as measured by the *National Journal* (with 0 = most conservative and 100 = most liberal); % Rural = percentage of member's district (for House)/state (for Senate) that is rural according to the U.S. census (1990); % White = percentage of member's district/state that is listed as white according to the U.S. census (1990); % College = percentage of the district/state with two or more years of college; Per Capita Income = per capita income of member's district/state, in thousands; % Vote for Clinton (1992) = percentage of member's district/state that voted for Bill Clinton in 1992; % Vote for Perot (1992) = percentage of member's district/state that voted for Ross Perot in 1992; % Vote in Last Election = percentage of the vote the member received in his/her most recent general election; Years Served = years that the legislator has served in the House or Senate; Party Unity Score = percentage of the time the member voted with a majority of his/her party against a majority of the other party, as compiled by *Congressional Quarterly*; Presidential Support Score = percentage of the time that the member supported the Clinton administration's position on a bill during the 103rd Congress (1993-1994), as compiled by *Congressional Quarterly*.

proposals in the Senate.

These findings should not come as much of a surprise because of the extreme partisan conflict over Clinton's proposal. Republicans saw the Clinton budget as a means of raising taxes and undoing the Reagan legacy that they revere. Democrats, though they were not enamored with the tax increases, felt that it was important to support the first Democratic president in 12 years. The result was a divide over the proposal that was along partisan and ideological lines.

The degree to which partisanship explains the support for the presidential budget in 1993 leads to another question–namely, what were the factors among congressional Democrats (since Republicans in Congress unanimously opposed the Clinton plan) that led them to support or oppose the plan of a president of their own party? Since partisanship was so dominant on the vote of the bill, this may be a more consequential consideration. Table 4.4 shows the means for the same ten factors analyzed in Table 4.3, but limiting the sample to only Democrats, comparing the characteristics of those Democrats who voted for the Clinton-supported 1993 bill and those who voted against it.

For House Democrats, the difference between the means for those who voted for and against the budget were statistically significant for all variables except the percentage of the vote the representative received in 1992–those who voted for the 1993 Budget Reconciliation Bill received approximately the same share of the vote in the 1992 elections as did those who voted against it–and the percentage of district with a college education. For Senate Democrats, the smaller number (56 total, 6 of whom opposed the Clinton budget) made for a less consistent pattern of differences between the two groups, but there were still statistically significant differences between the two groups in regards to ideology, one's vote share in his/her last election, party unity, and presidential support.

In the House, Democrats who voted for Clinton's proposed budget tended to be more liberal, to have served more terms, to be more supportive of the party and Clinton in general, and were elected from districts that more were more urban, had a higher proportion of minorities, were wealthier, gave Clinton a higher proportion of the vote in 1992, and gave Perot a lower share of the vote in 1992. In the Senate, Democrats who voted for the Clinton budget tended to be more liberal, more supportive of a majority of the party, and more supportive of Clinton's positions. They also received a lower percentage of the vote in their last election than those Democrats who opposed the 1993 Budget

Reconciliation Bill. Unquestionably, there were considerable differences between those districts that elected those Democrats who supported Clinton's budget proposal and those who voted against vote of the district was related to the member's vote on key budget votes during the 103rd Congress.

Thus, not only was the vote on the 1993 Budget Reconciliation Bill consistent with the partisan and ideological traits of individual members of Congress, but at the same time a member's vote on the budget was heavily influenced by the political beliefs of their district, as measured by presidential vote, as well as the demographics of the district. The characteristics of one's district therefore played an instrumental role in determining whether or not one would support the 1993 Budget Reconciliation Bill.

Political Consequences of the 1993 Budget Reconciliation Bill

The difficulty of the passage of the 1993 Budget Reconciliation Bill demonstrates the degree that members of Congress fear the electoral retribution for raising taxes. The anticipation of retrospective voting helps to focus legislative attention on the possible electoral consequences of voting to raise taxes even when they hear little from their constituents in advance of congressional action. Even though there was little evidence that members of Congress incurred significant electoral risks for approving new taxes prior to 1993, policymakers fear the potential consequences of voting for increased taxes.[32] As a result, Congress plans very carefully for tax increases. They plan the timing, devise and use processes that insulate them from interest groups, strategize to minimize the pain to voters, and build coalitions of support.[33]

The fact that not a single Republican in either chamber voted in support of the 1993 Budget indicates the degree of by which partisanship and ideology dominated the vote on the bill.[34] By embracing the plan, if only barely, congressional Democrats gambled on their political futures, betting that deficit reduction would improve the economy in the long-run and improve their reelection prospects. Since they passed the budget package without a single Republican vote, Democrats hoped that they would get sole credit for future success of the bill.

Democrats were buoyed by polls suggesting public support for deficit reduction, even at the cost of higher taxes. It was hoped by congressional Democrats that citizens may have come to realize that real deficit reduction would necessitate more taxes. After the Clinton budget

Table 4.5
Willingness to Pay the New Taxes of the
1993 Budget Reconciliation Bill

Question: Do you object to paying the new taxes, or not?

	Yes	No	No Opinion
Total	47	52	1
Sex			
Male	45	54	1
Female	48	51	1
Education			
College post-grad	33	67	0
College graduate	41	59	0
College inc.	77	20	3
No college	46	53	1
Politics			
Republicans	66	33	1
Democrats	26	74	0
Independents	49	50	1
Ideology			
Liberal	32	68	0
Moderate	39	61	0
Conservative	59	40	1
Income			
$50,000 and over	46	54	0
$30,000-49,999	47	52	1
$20,000-29,999	41	59	0
Under $20,000	49	50	1

Source: Gallup Poll (August 8-10, 1993; Survey GO 422004, Q.19). Based on national survey of 799 interviews. Poll number 335 of 1993.

was passed by Congress in August 1993, citizens were asked about the budget deal. Despite the bitter controversy over rising taxes, Americans were surprisingly willing to pay for the new levies called for in the budget plan. According to a Gallup Poll taken after the budget plan was implemented, 52 percent of the respondents said that they did not object to new taxes, and only 47 percent said that they objected. Of those who also claimed that the American public was partly to blame for the deficit, 60 percent said that they did not object to the tax increases (see Table 4.5). Not surprisingly, those who called themselves Democrats and liberals were much more supportive of the new taxes than were Republicans and conservatives. Interestingly, however, even though the new taxes were disproportionately on the wealthy, those with the lowest incomes were actually the least willing to support the new taxes and those with a college graduate education overwhelmingly supported the taxes.

Democratic optimism that the 1993 tax increases would not be a political hindrance, however, evaporated as the 1994 congressional elections approached. As the 1994 elections proved, the Democrats' support of tax increases did not help them politically.[35] Despite a relatively healthy economy in November 1994, Democrats who supported the Clinton economic plan did poorly in the midterm elections. Of the 228 House Democrats that sought reelection, 34 lost, including 28 who voted for the 1993 Budget Reconciliation Bill. More tellingly, not a single Republican incumbent lost a reelection bid for Congress in 1994. Even in an environment wherein voters were calling for deficit reduction, voting to raise taxes or cut programs proved to be a politically hazardous move for members of Congress.

The Success of the 1993 Budget Reconciliation Bill: The Advent of Budget Surpluses

Overall, the 1993 Budget Reconciliation Bill was expected to shrink, but not eliminate, the deficit. Annual deficits, however, shrank dramatically after the measure was enacted–indeed they shrank much more than anyone, including the Clinton administration, predicted. Every year during the Clinton administration the federal government produced a budget with a lower deficit or higher surplus. Though other factors, such as strong economic growth (which started at the end of the Bush administration) and the Federal Reserve Board's monetary policies under the direction of Alan Greenspan, undoubtably aided the cause of deficit reduction, the 1993 Budget Reconciliation Bill without question was remarkably successful in its goal of reducing the federal budget deficit. After the 1993 Budget became law, the effective tax rate on individual income increased notably, as Figure 4.1 demonstrates. As a result, the federal government saw a dramatic increase in revenues garnered from the individual income tax.[36]

Despite the unprecedented reduction of the federal budget deficit throughout his presidency, however, Clinton has seemingly garnered few political rewards for this achievement. The elimination of a federal budget deficit may have been Clinton's greatest accomplishment as president. Every year that Clinton was president, the economy flourished and the federal budget picture improved. President Clinton, however, was unable to sell the achievements of his budgetary blueprint during his presidency. According to one poll, 32 percent said that Clinton deserved no credit at all for balancing the budget. When asked who deserved more credit for reducing the deficit, the number who said Clinton was virtually even with the number who claimed Republicans in Congress.[37]

For most of his presidency, Clinton did not necessarily pursue a budgetary strategy consistent with produces budget surpluses. He did not commit to the concept of a balanced budget until 1995, and that was for budgets in the future, when he would be no longer be occupying the White House. Surpluses, however, arrived earlier because the strong economy produced an unexpected surge in revenues. Once the surplus did arrive, it dramatically changed the nature of the budget debate.

Once the reality of long-term surplus projections set in, the White House and congressional Republicans quickly laid claim to the revenues to finance their competing agendas. For Clinton, that included new spending on domestic programs and a new Medicare prescription drug benefit. Republicans, on the other hand, rallied behind tax cuts. Lawmakers, however, were nowhere near a consensus on how the extra revenues should be distributed.

The surplus allowed Clinton to pursue many of the goals that his administration had previously abandoned and put on hold. In health care and other social programs, Clinton at the end of his administration began to pursue the same goals as he sought at the beginning of this presidency in 1993, though usually by different means. For example, in 1993 Clinton proposed an expansion of the food stamp program and a Democratic Congress approved much of his proposal. The 1996 welfare law cut food stamp spending, but Clinton won restoration of some of the cuts in 1998 and in 2000 asked Congress to restore even more. Essentially, the surpluses of the end of his presidency allowed Clinton to successfully

Figure 4.1
Effective Tax Rate on Individual Income, Tax Years 1994-2000
(Percent)

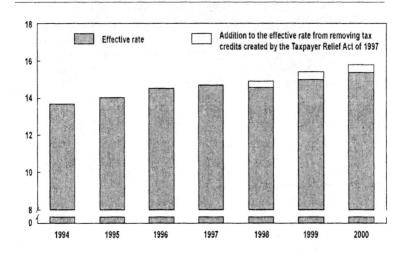

Source: Congressional Budget Office

adopt a more incremental approach in support of his policy goals.

Many Republicans, however, continued to believe that Congress should force the White House to bend to its will and supported a political strategy of avoiding surpluses. For example, Tom DeLay, the House majority whip, claimed that draining the surplus was a deliberate strategy designed to force President Clinton to submit to congressional Republicans' political will. The plan, DeLay said, was for Republicans to drain all of the surplus out of next year's budget and force President Clinton to pay for any of his additional spending requests out of the Social Security surplus, which both parties have pledged to protect. It was hoped that this strategy would force Clinton to sign the Republican spending bills or break his pledge to keep his hands off Social Security funds. From a public opinion perspective, however, it seemed as though President Clinton may have had the upper hand; the Republicans call for tax cuts did not resonate with the American public. When asked budget priorities, Americans appeared to desire increasing spending on domestic programs and reducing the national debt more than they were clamoring for tax cuts (see Chapter 6).

Although there were trillions of dollars in projected future surpluses, Congress and the White House cold not agree on what to do with the windfall of new projected revenues. There was no large tax cut nor an expansion in spending programs. Gridlock, however, had important policy consequences. It meant that the surplus was left intact. The result was that running a surplus automatically went to paying down the debt the nation had run up the previous three decades. Had the federal government continued on this course, it could have eliminated the national debt in 10 to 15 years. While this approach was never put to a vote or debated fully debated in Congress, it resulted in an outcome that most economists considered positive for the economy over the long run. As one economist argued, the nation is "at one of those times when doing nothing–or, at any rate, doing very little, is preferable to doing something."[38] Debt reduction was a fallback position, embraced by President Clinton to block the Republican effort to cut taxes after congressional Republicans refused to go along with Democrats calls for more government spending.

Conclusion

Congress has looked toward the President to lead the process of forming the national budget ever since the Budget and Accounting Act of 1921 made the president responsible for submitting a budget proposal to Congress. Yet, for the most part, presidents have tended to focus on other priorities. After he was elected president, Clinton proved to be an exception to this trend. Clinton proposed a politically risky budgetary blueprint that relied heavily on increased taxes–what was to become the 1993 Budget Reconciliation Bill. An analysis of the congressional vote on the 1993 Budget Reconciliation Bill displays the extreme partisan conflict over the proposal. Party and ideology were the primary factors determining one's vote on the budget. Furthermore, the significant differences between the districts among those who supported the 1993 Budget Reconciliation Bill and those who opposed it, both demographically and politically, demonstrates the potential effects of the constituency and representation on the budget process. Without a vote to spare, Clinton was able to get Congressional approval of his budget blueprint in an extremely partisan environment.

With the help of a strong economy, the 1993 Budget Reconciliation Bill was extraordinary successful in what it set out to do: reduce the federal budget deficit. The elimination of nearly 30 years of federal budget deficits was undoubtably a remarkable achievement. Americans who have been so accustomed to political discourse over how to reduce the deficit found themselves encountering presidential candidates in 2000 debating how to spend a budget surplus. Interestingly, Americans facing a possible budget surplus for the first time in nearly 30 years were only lukewarm at best to the idea of tax cuts; more people were found to back paying down the federal debt than were found to back tax cuts.[39] Following public opinion on this matter would have been consistent with the General Accounting Office's position that "until the fiscal path for a period of budget surpluses is fully and clearly articulated there is a risk of losing the opportunity to enhance our long-term economic well-being."[40]

President George W. Bush undoubtedly faced a much rosier budget picture than that inherited by Clinton when he was elected president. As a result, Bush was able to get Congress to pass significant tax cuts after winning office. When Clinton assumed the presidency, the budget deficit was a central fact of life which limited what the federal government could do. New spending projects were taboo. With the deficit temporarily eliminated, it was possible to once again have a debate over whether the federal government should do more or cut taxes. With Bush's victory, tax cuts were enacted. With the resulting ballooning budget deficits, the arguments over what to do with large budget surpluses became moot.

Endnotes

1. Aaron Wildavsky and Namoi Caiden, *The New Politics of the Budgetary Process*, 4th ed. (New York: Longman, 2001), chapter 2.

2. Bernard Pitsvada, "The Executive Budget–An Idea Whose Time Has Passed," *Public Budgeting and Finance*, Spring 1988: 85-94.

3. Allen Schick, *Congress and Money* (Washington, D.C.: AEI, 1980), chapter 2.

4. Ibid.

5. Allen Schick, *The Capacity to Budget* (Washington, D.C.: The Urban Institute, 1990), p. 162.

6. Ibid., p. 167.

7. Donald F. Kettl, *Deficit Politics* (New York: Longman, 2003), p. 130.

8. Ibid., p. 133.

9. Irene Rubin, *The Politics of Public Budgeting* (Chatham, NJ: Chatham House, 1990), p. 64.

10. Dennis Ippolito, *Congressional Spending* (Ithaca: Cornell University Press, 1981), p. 167.

11. Ibid., p. 9.

12. Jeffrey Cohen, Michael Krassa and John Hamman, "The Impact of Presidential Campaigning on Midterm U.S. Senate Elections," *American Political Science Review* 85 (1991): 165-178.

13. Douglas Rivers and Nancy Rose, "Passing the President's Program: Public Opinion and Presidential Influence in Congress," *American Journal of Political Science* 29 (1985): 183-196.

14. Robert Lee and Ronald Johnson, *Public Budgeting Systems* 5th ed. (Gaithersburg, MD: Aspen Publishers, 1994), pp. 17 and 117.

15. Steven Schier, *A Decade of Deficits* (Albany: SUNY Press, 1992), pp. 46-47.

16. Chuck Alston, "The Figuring Behind the Figures," *Congressional Quarterly* (February 20, 1993), p. 356.

17. George Hager, "Time Bombs for Clinton Seen in Bush's Final Budget," *Congressional Quarterly* (January 9, 1993), pp. 68-72.

18. Lance Leloup, *Budgetary Politics* (Brunswick, OH: King's Court Press, 1977), p. 126.

19. George Hager and David Cloud, "Clinton Team's Similar Lines Focus on Deficit Reduction," *Congressional Quarterly* (February 20, 1993), pp. 120-123.

20. George Hager, "President Throws Down Gauntlet," *Congressional Quarterly* (February 20, 1993), p. 356.

21. David Cloud, "Package of Tax Increases Reverses GOP Approach," *Congressional Quarterly* (February 20, 1993), p. 361.

22. George Hager and David Cloud, "Democrats Tie Their Fate to Clinton Budget Bill," *Congressional Quarterly* (August 7, 2003, 1993), p. 2122.

23. George Hager and David Cloud, "Democrats Pull Off Squeaker in Approving Clinton Plan," *Congressional Quarterly* (May 29, 1993), p. 1341.

24. Lee and Johnson (1994).

25. George Edwards, *Presidential Influence in Congress* (San Francisco: W.H. Freeman and Company, 1980).

26. Michael Mezey, *Congress, the President, and Public Policy* (Boulder: Westview Press, 1989).

27. John Kindgon, *Congressmen's Voting Decisions*, 3rd ed. (Ann Arbor: University of Michigan Press, 1989).

28. Edwards (1980).

29. E. Scott Alder, "Constituency Characteristics and the 'Guardian' Model of Appropriations Subcommittees 1959-1998," *American Journal of Political Science* 44 (2000): 104-114; Benjamin Page, Robert Y. Shapiro, Paul W. Gronke, and Robert M. Rosenberg, "Constituency, Party, and Representation in Congress," *Public Opinion Quarterly* 48 (1984): 741-756; Aage Clausen, *How Congressmen Decide: A Policy Focus* (New York: St. Martin's Press, 1973); W. Wayne Shannon, *Party, Constituency and Congressional Voting* (Baton Rouge: LSU Press, 1968).

30. Edwards (1980), pp. 108-110.

31. Barbara Sinclair, "House Majority Party Leadership in an Era of Divided Control," *Congress Reconsidered*, 5th ed., Lawrence Dodd and Bruce Oppenheimer eds., pp. 237-258 (Washington: CQ Press, 1993); Steven Smith, "Forces of Change in Senate Party Leadership and Organization," *Congress Reconsidered*, 5th ed., Lawrence Dodd and Bruce Oppenheimer eds., pp. 259-290 (Washington: CQ Press, 1993).

32. R. Douglas Arnold, *The Logic of Congressional Action* (New Haven: Yale University Press, 1990).

33. Rubin (1990).

34. Patrick Fisher, "The Prominence of Partisanship in the Congressional Budget Process," *Party Politics* 5 (1999): 225-236.

35. Linda Killian, *The Freshmen* (Boulder, CO: Westview, 1998).

36. Patrick Fisher, "The Success of the 1993 Budget Reconciliation Bill at Reducing the Federal Budget Deficit," *The Review of Policy Research* 19 (2002): 30-43.

37. Susan Page and William M. Welch, "Poll: Don't Use Surplus to Cut Taxes," *USA Today* (January 16, 1998), pp. 1A and 6A.

38. Robert J. Samuelson, "Let Them Be Lame Ducks," *Newsweek* (February 7, 2000), p. 30.

39. Page and Welch (1998).

40. General Accounting Office, *Budget Surpluses: Experiences of Other Nations and Implications for the United States* (Washington: GAO Press, 2000).

Chapter 5

Partisanship and the Congressional Budget Process

By defining alternatives, political parties are potentially decisive in determining budget priorities and outcomes. Because they are the only organizations that can win elections on a widespread scale, the parties have a monopoly. The parties organize the electorate by reducing the voters' alternatives to the extreme limit of simplification.[1] The United States, however, tends to have parties that are weak by comparative standards. This has the potential to cause problems in terms of congressional budgeting. A sense of collective responsibility is necessary to produce balanced and fair budgets. Even though the parties in Congress are relatively weak, however, they are far from irrelevant. More than any other single factor, partisanship determines a member's budgetary actions.

Party affiliation is an important factor in congressional voting decisions, and it can be used to explain much of the voting behavior of Congress. It has been found that political control of Congress influences budgetary outcomes, with Democrats giving higher priority to domestic spending programs than Republicans, especially for programs that benefit the poor.[2] Even though political parties in Congress tend to be much more distinctive than party members in the electorate, it does not follow that congressional party leaders have a powerful influence on a member's votes. Even though congressional colleagues are a powerful influence upon member voting, party leaders have little extra influence beyond that of ordinary members of Congress. This is in part due to the fact that party leaders tend to have only weak powers, especially when it comes to sanctioning members who stray too much from the party line. Party leaders, though, can be seen as reliable barometers that indicate to members which way the wind is blowing on an issue.

Political Parties and the Electorate

Though the weakness of the American political parties is probably the result of the country's fragmented political institutions more than anything else, it is also true that the American people are not an overly ideological people, possibly enhancing the weak-party standard. Historically, there has been a strong ideological consensus in American society and there have really been no other alternatives to classical liberalism[3] Many contend that an essential strength in the United States lies in the fact that it is essentially nonideological and its two-party system subsumes all major streams of thought within the classical liberal tradition. Americans are not comfortable with terminology that is linked to ideological imagery.[4] To advocates of government responsiveness, however, public policy alterations based upon ideological beliefs are viewed as a positive development because the election process can serve to select leaders who advocate specific philosophies which shape policy. Ideology reflected in popular politics thus triumphs over technocratic values. Ideology, however, can pose a threat to objective policymaking. Ideological blinders can have an extremely negative influence on society if they prevent policymakers from carrying out objective analysis of problems.[5] This may have been the case over the Clinton deficit-reduction measures found in the 1993 Budget Reconciliation Bill, which saw conservatives immediately condemn the package even though it sought to reduce the budget, something that conservatives traditionally have strongly advocated, because they preferred to have it done in a different way (i.e., more spending cuts, less tax increases).

Even though some ideological basis for justifying the beliefs and actions of members of Congress is probably necessary when dealing with the budget, it is also true that be acting ideologically they can irritate the people they represent. It has been found that large portions of the electorate do not have meaningful ideological beliefs, even on issues that receive considerable media attention. Very substantial portions of the public simply do not fall along any ideological dimension at all.[6] While citizens may not have consistent belief systems, however, it does not follow that they are not partisan. Party identification is the single best predictor of how a person votes, though there has been a weakening of party attachments as candidates increasingly avoid party labels while campaigning. More specifically, party identification is a significant factor in people's spending views. Congressional Democrats are likely to favor more spending in just about every area than are Republicans, with the exception of defense.

The United States is a heterogeneous nation. There are a great variety of economic and social interests, classes, ethnic groups, religious groups and regional interests in this country. As a result, American parties must be "big tents" so as to build majorities–they must incorporate many different people, views and beliefs. This makes the parties within Congress especially fragile enterprises. The differences that separate groups and regions from each other are only somewhat bridged over by the parties, making congressional budgeting a very difficult task.

Political Parties and Congress

Despite the appearance of party power, voting on crucial budget issues often crosses party lines and violates party pledges and platforms. In some ways party dominates, yet the effect of party effort and loyalty is often negligible.[7] At the most, the congressional parties are tied to the rest of their parties by some agreement on an inarticulate ideology of common interests, attitudes, and loyalties. There exists no mechanism by which parties can establish control over and responsibility for their actions in Congress. Instead, parties are divided by the separation of powers structure and federalism's regionalistic peculiarities fundamental to American government, as well as differing goals and commitments.[8] These factors may make it more difficult to come to agreement on the difficult budgetary issues that divide legislators. Members of Congress tend to be attracted to a particular party more because of its promise as a mechanism for moving into government than as a mechanism for governing and budgeting. An elemental truth of party politics in the United States is that parties are simply a way of organizing activists and supporters to make a bid for office.[9]

Party labels, however, reveal quite a bit about members of Congress. On some issues, such as budgeting, there are considerable differences on party stands on the issues. Voters, however, do not reward party loyalty, so when constituency demands and party demands conflict, the desires of the constituency will usually determine a member's actions. Nevertheless, party affiliation is the most important single factor in predicting how members will respond to issues–the essential fact to know about any member is his or her partisanship.[10] Yet, despite the relative importance of party cohesion, the fact remains that the parties in Congress achieve only modest levels of cohesion. Party lines are often obliterated in the coalitions that enact important legislation.[11]

Thus, party loyalty does not govern the behavior of members, but it is also not a factor to be taken lightly. Since the 1980s there has been a marked rise in partisanship of both houses of Congress. This partisanship has extended to relations with the executive branch. The relationship between Congress and the White House has become more confrontational (in a large part due to the frequency of divided government) as Congress is more and more frequently choosing political options that the president opposes.[12] Overall, the proportion of roll-call votes in Congress in which the parties oppose each other is not particularly large compared to other countries. The congressional budget process, however, has become an increasingly partisan and acrimonious process since the Reagan administration. Today, to a large degree, the parties different approaches to the budget define what it means to be a Republican and a Democrat.

Political Parties and Congressional Budgeting

Minimal partisanship, it has been argued, is a necessary condition of committee integration and extreme partisanship represents one of the most serious disruptive conditions.[13] There has been a significant increase in partisan disputes over fiscal policy since 1966, a time when a much wider budgetary consensus existed. In its struggle to establish fiscal policy and improve its control of the national budget, sharp disputes have developed in Congress on the direction of fiscal policy, especially over the deficit.

That votes on budget resolutions and major spending items have become more partisan can be seen by the vote on the 1993 Budget Reconciliation Bill, where not a single Republican in Congress voted for President Clinton's budgetary blueprint. As the debate over the 1993 budget exemplifies, differences in the budget have increasingly come to define the differences between the parties, with the Republicans becoming the vehement anti-tax party and the Democrats, by default, the anti-deficit party. The increase of political polarization has lead Congress to devote much more time and effort to budgeting. There is much more understanding of spending, taxing, and the relationship between them in Congress today. Understanding, however, does not equal agreement.

While all members of Congress say that they favor a balanced budget, the parties differ greatly on how to accomplish this goal. The degree of attitude constraint and voting consistency on fiscal issues appears to be much greater than in other areas. Democrats tend to be more disposed toward keeping as much social spending as possible in today's budgetary environment even if that means higher taxes. Republicans, on the other hand, desire lower taxes more than social spending (though they do tend to be pro-spending when it comes to the defense). Thus, the Democrats favor relatively high expenditures and high revenues, while the Republicans favor relatively low expenditures and low revenues. Balancing the budget at lower levels of expenditures and revenues is quite different than balancing taxing and spending at higher levels.[14]

In terms of economic policy, both Democrats and Republicans tend to support policies that are often not conducive to balancing the budget. Most Democrats tend to favor a Keynesian countercyclical budget policy that makes redistribution an ongoing achievement of stabilization. The Republican alternative bases its growth hopes upon the supply-side effects of reductions in personal marginal income tax rates. For Republicans, supply-side economics promises short-term stabilization effects as well as the long-held goal of smaller government. In this way Republicans can avoid the problem of colliding allocation beliefs (limit government) and stabilization tactics (support countercyclical spending).[15] Yet, despite the popularity of Ronald Reagan as president, the political as well as policy success of supply-side economics is still very much in doubt. When Bob Dole proposed a major tax reduction after winning the Republican presidential nomination in 1996, for example, his proposals were met with general skepticism and failed to be a vote winner. Why did Dole's tax cut proposals fall flat? One reason may be that the proposed tax cuts were linked to the tax cuts of 1981, which lead to massive budget deficits. The "mistakes of 1981" were not to be repeated.[16] After being elected president in 2000, however, George W. Bush was able to enact a tax-cuts following Reagan's supply-side model, demonstrating that advocates of supply-side economic policies who believe that tax cuts are more important than balancing the budget still have a prominent role in the Republican party.

Nothing in postwar fiscal policy making has caused more conflict between Democrats and Republicans than taxes. This conflict arises because revenue is viewed not only as fuel for government spending, but also as an economic stimulus all on its own. The consequences of taxing decisions, needless to say, produce an enormous impact on the budget. It has been estimated, for example, that the Economic Recovery Tax Act of 1981 cost the federal government $2,098 billion from in lost revenue over the period 1982-1991.[17]

The large deficits of the 1980s recast American politics. Traditionally, the Republicans have been seen as the anti-deficit party, but since the Reagan administration the emphasis of the party has been more on cutting taxes than cutting the deficit. Beginning with Walter Mondale's run for the presidency in 1984 the Democrats became the anti-deficit party, moving away from the Keynesian position that dominated the economic beliefs of the party in the postwar era. Furthermore, Republicans began to see the deficit as not so bad because it tended to favor creditors, mainly Republican, over debtors, mainly Democrats. Thus, by 1984 a plausible constituency-based argument supported Democratic concern about deficits.[18]

This trend can be seen worldwide. Traditionally, parties of the political left (the Labour Party in Great Britain, for example) have tended to be more likely to run larger deficits than were parties of the right. Since the 1970s, however, the association of partisanship to deficits may be less clear. The supply-side economic policies of some governments on the right have produced very large deficits, while Socialist and Social Democratic governments increasingly have adopted rather conservative fiscal policies. Overall, the political persuasion of a government appears to have little relationship to deficits, with several conservative governments (Netherlands, Canada) producing large deficits and several social democratic governments (Finland, Sweden) producing relatively small deficits.[19]

The Increased Partisanship of Budget Process

In the past two decades, Congress has found it difficult to reach agreement on the budget because of the sharp partisan divisions over fiscal policy. The partisan character of the congressional budget process can be seen by looking at votes on congressional budget resolutions since the large Reagan tax cuts of the early 1980s. It is through the budget resolution that Congress states its budget priorities for the next fiscal

Table 5.1
Partisanship on Budget Resolution Votes
House of Representatives

Fiscal Year	Total Yes-No	Democrats Yes-No	Republicans Yes-No	Rice Index of Cohesion		
				Total	Democrats	Republicans
1983	219-206	63-174	156-32	3.0	46.8	66.0
1984	229-196	225-36	4-160	7.8	72.4	95.2
1985	250-168	229-29	21-139	19.6	77.6	73.8
1986	258-170	234-15	24-155	20.6	88.0	72.2
1987	245-179	228-19	17-166	13.0	84.6	81.4
1988	215-201	212-34	3-167	3.4	72.4	96.4
1989	319-102	227-24	92-78	51.6	80.8	8.2
1990	263-157	157-96	106-61	25.2	19.6	27.0
1991	218-208	218-34	0-174	2.2	73.0	100
1992	261-163	243-17	18-145	23.0	86.8	78.0
1993	209-207	209-47	0-159	0.4	63.2	100
1994	243-183	242-11	0-172	14.0	91.4	100
1995	223-175	222-11	0-164	12.0	90.6	100
1996	238-193	8-191	230-1	10.4	92.0	99.1
1997	226-195	5-190	221-4	4.9	94.9	96.4
1998	333-99	132-72	201-26	54.2	29.4	77.1
1999	216-204	3-194	213-9	2.3	97.0	92.0
2000	221-208	4-205	217-2	3.0	96.2	98.2
	AVERAGE (1983-1995):			15.1	72.9	76.8
	AVERAGE (1996-2000):			15.0	81.9	92.6
	AVERAGE (1983-2000):			15.0	75.4	81.2

Source: Roll call votes are from *Congressional Quarterly Almanac*, various years; Rice Index of Cohesion compiled by author. The Rice Index of Cohesion is measured by subtracting the percentage against a bill (the budget resolutions in this case) from the percentage for the bill. The Rice Index is then expressed as the absolute difference between the two percentage figures.

Table 5.2
Partisanship on Budget Resolution Votes
Senate

Fiscal Year	Total Yes-No	Democrats Yes-No	Republicans Yes-No	Rice Index of Cohesion Total	Democrats	Republicans
1983	49-43	3-41	46-2	6.6	86.4	91.6
1984	50-49	29-17	21-32	1.0	26.0	20.8
1985	41-34	1-31	40-3	9.4	93.8	86.0
1986	50-49	1-45	48-4	1.0	95.6	85.6
1987	70-25	38-6	32-19	47.4	82.8	25.4
1988	53-46	50-3	3-43	7.0	88.6	87.0
1989	69-26	44-6	25-20	45.2	76.0	11.2
1990	68-31	38-17	30-14	37.4	38.2	36.4
1991		Voice Vote		----	----	----
1992	57-41	49-7	8-34	16.4	75.0	72.0
1993	52-41	36-16	16-25	12.0	71.4	22.0
1994	55-45	55-2	0-43	10.0	92.0	100
1995	53-46	51-4	2-42	7.0	85.4	95.4
1996	57-42	3-42	54-0	15.1	86.7	100
1997	53-46	0-46	53-0	9.0	100	100
1998	78-22	37-8	41-14	56.0	64.4	49.1
1999	57-41	3-41	54-0	16.2	86.4	100
2000	55-44	1-44	54-0	11.1	96.6	100

	AVERAGE (1983-1995):			16.7	75.9	61.1
	AVERAGE (1996-2000):			19.0	86.8	89.8
	AVERAGE (1983-2000):			17.1	79.1	70.0

Source: Roll call votes are from *Congressional Quarterly Almanac*, various years; Rice Index of Cohesion compiled by author. The Rice Index of Cohesion is measured by subtracting the percentage against a bill (the budget resolutions in this case) from the percentage for the bill. The Rice Index is then expressed as the absolute difference between the two percentage figures.

year.   Traditionally, budget resolutions tended to be relatively nonpartisan.[20]   Since 1983, however, the margins by which budget resolutions have passed the House and the Senate have been extremely partisan in nature. Using the Rice Index of Cohesion[21] to measure the degree of cohesion among Democrats and Republicans in both the House and Senate, one finds a high degree of polarization in the budget process (see Tables 5.1 and 5.2). When the Democrats controlled the House during the budget resolutions for fiscal years 1983-1995, the Rice Index of Cohesion for the Democrats was 72.9 and for the Republicans it was 76.8. Since the Republicans took control of the House after the 1994 elections, the parties have become even more united against one another on budget priorities. For the budget resolutions in which the Republicans have been in the majority (since 1996), the Democrats had a Rice Index of 81.9 and the Republicans 92.6. The Senate has historically been less partisan on budget resolutions than the House, yet from 1983-2000 Senate Democrats had a Rice Index of 79.1 and Senate Republicans 70.0, similar figures to those in the House. Furthermore, since the Republicans took control of the Senate after the 1994 elections the partisanship on budget resolutions in the Senate has increased significantly, to the point that there is now no noticeable difference with the House. In both the House and the Senate the parties have never differed so greatly on their taxing and spending preferences.

Constituency pressures associated with the budget appear to be significantly higher in the House than Senate. The electoral consequences of voting for a budget resolution are much more salient for members of the House.[22] This may help explain why the House has found it difficult to reach agreement on budget policy because of sharp partisan division over deficits and fiscal policy. The arguments between Democrats and Republicans in the House Budget Committee are often replayed on the House floor where Republicans, unable to reduce spending totals in the Budget Committee, offer substitute budget resolutions. The House Budget Committee's mixed record in defending its resolutions from floor amendments has complicated the budget process considerably. The Senate Budget Committee has led a less precarious existence than its House counterpart, but it still has had to defend its resolutions against more and more amendments each year. For the most part, however, the Senate Committee's bipartisanship has enabled the Senate to focus on long-term budget control strategies better than the House.[23]

Policy partisanship tends to be greater in the House than the Senate. This is in a large part due to institutional construct. In the House, the rules are designed so that the majority party can work its will, while in the Senate the ability of the majority to act in an overtly partisan fashion is severely limited. Thus, the level of party voting seems to be strongly affected by established institutional arrangements. Until the 1980s, for example, Senate budget resolutions tended to be bipartisan, even though in the House they were often highly partisan.[23]

Yet, as the data in Table 5.1 and Table 5.2 demonstrate, since 1983 the margins by which budget resolutions have passed the House are similar to the margins by which they have passed in the Senate. There does tend to be a slightly higher degree of agreement in the Senate on budget resolutions than can be found in the House. When the budget resolutions are divided by party, however, it is found that while Democrats in the Senate were more cohesive than Democrats in the House, the opposite was found among Republicans; Republicans in the House actually tended to be more in agreement among themselves on budget resolutions than Senate Republicans. Thus, despite the Senate's tradition of seeking a bipartisan approach to budget resolutions, recent votes on budget resolutions appear to differ little between the House and Senate; the budget resolutions have been highly partisan in both chambers of Congress.

In the Senate, the Democrats tended to be more in agreement on the Senate side of the aisle while the Republicans showed a greater degree of cohesiveness in the House. This may be the result of the possibility that those in the minority (the Republicans were in the minority in the House during the whole period while the Democrats were in the minority in the Senate from 1981-1987) are more likely to be in ideological agreement because of their relatively smaller numbers.

The nature of the institution suggests that the Senate consistently should be more moderate ideologically than the House. The Founding Fathers, after all, intended that the Senate act as a moderating force that would generally protect the status quo. On budgetary matters for the past two decades, however, this has definitely not been the case, indicating that the Senate can be, when the conditions are right, an extremely partisan body.

Why is the Congressional Budget Process so Partisan?

The two most significant pressures members of Congress face when it comes to decisions on the budget are the constituency and political party. Even though these are two supposedly distinct variables, the two variables are not unequivocally separated. The selection of Democrats and Republicans in congressional elections is highly associated with certain socio-economic characteristics of the various constituencies.[25] It has been found, however, that while constituency factors play an important part in determining vote choice, the party factor tends to be strong enough that similar districts do not have similar voting records when their member's are from opposite parties.[26] That is, members of Congress of opposite parties, even though they were representing districts with similar demographic characteristics, had dissimilar voting records: one was supportive of the Democratic position and the other was supportive of the Republican position.

The important role the parties, as well as sectional cleavages, play today in American politics can be seen in Table 5.3, which displays the differences between some of the major cleavages that exist today in American politics. Table 5.3 portrays what a mean Democratic district looks like, both in terms of legislative behavior and district demographic/political characteristics compared to a district that has elected a Republican to Congress (for a discussion of the variables analyzed, see Chapter 1). Unquestionably, there are substantial differences between both the demographic/political characteristics of the districts as well as the type of representation they receive, especially in the House.

Democrats in the House tend to be overwhelmingly more liberal ideologically and, during the Clinton presidency, were much more likely to support the positions of President Clinton than were Republicans. House Democrats also tend to come from districts that have significantly more minorities, have fewer people that attended college, have lower per capita income, and gave Democratic presidential candidates a higher percentage of the vote. They also tended to come from districts that gave Perot a lower share of the vote in the 1992 presidential election than did those from Republican districts. In terms of party unity, percentage of the vote in one's last election, and seniority in Congress, however, there was only a negligible difference–both Republicans and Democrats alike were very similar in these respects.

Like House Democrats, Senate Democrats tended to be substantially more liberal and more supportive of Clinton's policies during his presidency. Democratic senators also tended to come from states that gave Clinton a higher share of the vote and Perot a lower proportion of the vote than Republican senators. Unlike the House, however, state demographics were not revealing predictors of partisan discrepancies.

Congressional Budgeting: A Representational Perspective

Table 5.3
A Comparison of Democratic and Republican Districts
House and Senate

	House Democrats	House Republicans	Senate Democrats	Senate Republicans
Ideology	69.84	21.59***	70.64	24.02***
% Rural	23.34	26.99	29.86	34.36
% White	70.08	84.03***	82.13	85.84
% College	42.93	47.94***	44.29	46.36
Per Capita Income	13.59	15.68***	13.95	13.25
% Vote for Clinton (1992)	49.09	35.90***	43.02	38.89***
% Vote for Perot (1992)	17.15	20.42***	18.64	21.41**
% Vote in Last Election	64.25	62.16	61.02	59.55
Years Served	10.88	10.08	10.96	11.55
Party Unity Score	88.88	87.39	85.57	85.59
Presidential Support Score	79.17	44.64***	88.77	37.43***

*p < .05; **p < .01; ***p < .001

Each figure represents the mean total of all Democrats and Republicans in the House and Senate respectively.

Definition of Variables: Ideology = member's ideological score, as measured by the *National Journal* (with 0 = most conservative and 100 = most liberal); % Rural = percentage of member's district (for House)/state (for Senate) that is rural according to the U.S. census (1990); % White = percentage of member's district/state that is listed as white according to the U.S. census (1990); % College = percentage of the district/state with two or more years of college; Per Capita Income = per capita income of member's district/state, in thousands; % Vote for Clinton (1992) = percentage of member's district/state that voted for Bill Clinton in 1992; % Vote for Perot (1992) = percentage of member's district/state that voted for Ross Perot in 1992; % Vote in Last Election = percentage of the vote the member received in his/her most recent general election; Years Served = years that the legislator has served in the House or Senate; Party Unity Score = percentage of the time the member voted with a majority of his/her party against a majority of the other party, as compiled by *Congressional Quarterly*; Presidential Support Score = percentage of the time that the member supported the Clinton administration's position on a bill during the 103rd Congress (1993-1994), as compiled by *Congressional Quarterly*.

This suggests that the partisanship of the budget process in recent years may be the result of the representational nature of Congress. Congressional districts represented by Democratic members of Congress, as born out by the data in Table 5.3, tend to be significantly different demographically and politically than those districts represented by Republicans; Republicans and Democrats are elected from distinctly different constituencies. This dynamic has the potential to dramatically influence the manner in which Congress attempts to budget. The experiences of congressional attempts to produce a federal budget the past three decades support the contention that increased partisanship has indeed altered the dynamics of the congressional budget process. In the process of representing the view's of their constituents, members of Congress are moving toward very different budget priorities.

Of particular interest when it comes to budget priorities is the per capita income of the district. Republican districts are wealthier than Democratic districts and the per capita income of House districts is correlated with the House member's ideology. Are the political parties advocating class-based budget preferences of their constituents? The parties different stances regarding what to do with the budget surplus may in fact be class based. While Democrats have argued for using the surplus for programs such as Social Security, Medicare, and education, the Republicans have proposed major tax cuts that they acknowledged would mostly benefit the affluent. The policies thus proposed by each party will vary greatly by class. Tax cuts may give some monetary benefits to the less affluent but at the same time they will deprive government of resources for programs beneficial to those with lower-incomes.[26]

As Table 5.4 displays, the parties support by class has changed significantly the past five decades. The Democrats have long been held to have disproportionate support from those with lower incomes, but the partisan differences of those with higher and lower incomes has continued to increase since the 1950s, despite common belief to the contrary.[27] The bottom third economically voted 22 percent more Democratic than the economic top third in the 1990s, more than twice what the differential between the bottom and top thirds in the 1950s and 1960s.

The increased partisanship of the congressional budget process may be a result of the fact that the Democrats have received an increasing amount of support from those with lower incomes at the expense of the Republicans. Democratic and Republican constituencies are pulling their representatives in opposite ways. Republican constituencies desire tax cuts because they would benefit the most from current tax cut

Table 5.4
Partisanship by Income Group:
Percent Voting Democratic for the House of Representatives
Within Bottom and Top Third of Income Groups by Decade

	Bottom Third	*Top Third*	*Difference*
1950s	57	47	10
1960s	60	53	7
1970s	66	52	13
1980s	68	51	17
1990s	66	44	22

Source: NES Cumulative File 1948-1998; Jeffrey M. Stonecash *Class and Party in American Politics* (Boulder, CO: Westview), p. 110.

proposals that emphasize reducing taxes on higher incomes. The fact that Republican tax cut proposals disproportionately would aid those with higher-incomes is simply a response to the constituency that elects them to office. For Democratic representatives, on the other hand, as those from higher incomes become a smaller proportion of the coalition that elects them to office, they may be less inclined to support tax reductions that would benefit this group.

The different approaches of congressional Democrats and Republicans can therefore be regarded as a result of the fact that Democrats and Republicans tend to follow the wishes of those partisans that elected them to office. Members of Congress may be simply responding to different portions of their constituencies.[28] This can be seen in looking at partisan budgetary preferences of voters in the 2000 presidential elections. There were significant partisan and ideological differences regarding taxing and spending proposals throughout the Clinton years that played a major role in the 2000 presidential elections. An exit poll of the 2000 presidential elections found that voters for Al Gore and George W. Bush advocated noticeably different priorities for the new president. Gore supporters argued that tax cuts should be a low priority for the new president while Bush supporters strongly supported tax cuts. Of those who claimed that tax cuts should be the top priority

Figure 5.1
Top Priority for New President

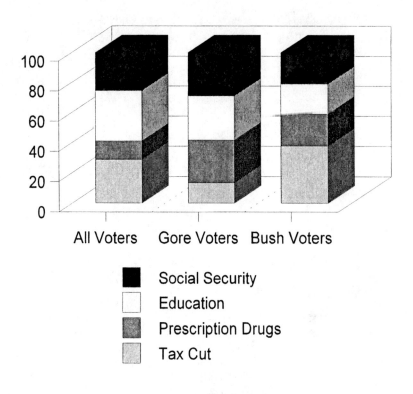

Source: Gallup Exit Poll of 2000 Elections of 13,130 voters nationwide
November 7, 2000.

for the next president, 70% voted for Bush. Of those who claimed that prescription drugs, education, and Social Security should be the top priority, most cast their votes for Gore (see Figure 5.1). This may explain why Bush made tax cuts the major focus of his new administration despite public opinion polls that showed that the American public tended to be ambivalent toward the necessity of reducing taxes.

Table 5.5
Partisan Differences on Surplus

"Some lawmakers are saying there will be a budget surplus in the coming years. If that happens and you had to choose between the following things, how would you like the money to be used?"

	All	*Republicans*	*Democrats*	*Independents*
Cut Income Taxes	13%	21%	7%	13%
Pay Down Debt	18%	23%	16%	16%
Preserve Medicare/ Social Security	54%	41%	68%	53%
Something Else (volunteered)	7%	6%	4%	10%
Combination (volunteered)	6%	8%	4%	6%
Don't Know	2%	1%	1%	2%

Source: CBS News/New York Times Poll of 947 adults nationwide May 10-13, 2000. Margin of error +/-3 percentage points.

When the government was producing a large budget surplus in 2000, there were significant differences between self-described Democrats and Republicans as to what to do with the surplus. Republicans were much more likely to support cutting income taxes and slightly more likely to support paying down the national debt while Democrats were much more likely to support using the surplus to preserve Medicare and Social Security, as Table 5.5 displays. Among Democrats, 68% said that they would like the surplus to be used for Social Security and only 7% for cutting income taxes. Among Republicans, more wanted the money to be used for Social Security (41%) than for any other option presented, but considerably more Republicans (21%) than Democrats (7%) said the surplus should be used to cut income taxes.

Which Party is More Likely to Support Deficit Reduction?

Almost all members of Congress claim to be against budget deficits and favor balancing the federal budget, at least in the abstract. When it comes to supporting the actual policies that would lead to expenditures and revenues being in balance, however, federal legislators often abandon balanced budget principles. Who, then, are the true "deficit hawks" in Congress? That is, which members of Congress are most likely to consistently support policies leading to balanced budgets? What characteristics differentiate those legislators who are more likely to support long-term debt reduction?

A popular explanation for the inability of Congress to consistently produce balanced budgets is that members of Congress are unwilling to make tough choices, thus undermining the budget process. If Congress was willing to cut spending or raise taxes, the deficit problem would abate and the process would stabilize.[29] Politically, however, supporting legislation that reduces spending or raises taxes is perceived to be dangerous.

Making life difficult for legislators is the fact that the American public tends to have contradictory opinions on the necessity of a balanced budget. They tend to be critical of government spending from a conceptual perspective, but at the same time welcome it for specific programs. Democracy confounds the budget process because it is believed that spending money helps one electorally and imposing costs by raising taxes is politically harmful.

Yet, since most members of Congress publicly argue that they are against large budget deficits, it is difficult to assess specifically who in Congress is to blame for deficit spending. Accountability becomes a problem—who is to blame for large budget deficits?

One measurement of the degree by which legislators support the difficult political compromises that must be made in order to regularly produce balanced budgets is the annual "Fiscal Responsibility" scores given to members of both the House and the Senate by the Concord Coalition, an organization dedicated to balancing the federal budget. Budgetary accountability is the guiding principle behind the Concord Coalition's ratings of members of Congress.

The Concord Coalition is an anti-deficit group whose official mission is "to challenge national office holders to make the tough political choices required to balance the federal budget and keep it in balance."[30] It was formed as a reaction against the massive budget deficits that were annually plaguing the national government throughout the 1980s and early

1990s. The Concord Coalition was founded in 1992–a year in which the deficit reached a record peacetime high of $290 billion–by the late Senator Paul Tsongas (D-MA), former Senator Warren Rudman (R-NH), and former Secretary of the Commerce Pete Peterson. Former Senator Sam Nunn (D-GA) joined Senator Rudman as the co-chairman of the Coalition in 1997 and was replaced by former Senator Robert Kerrey (D-NB) in 2001.

The Concord Coalition purports that it is standing up for the general interest by advocating fiscal responsibility and reform of entitlement programs to ensure their viability and fairness for future generations. Legislators often get a contradictory message from voters: cut taxes, do not reduce benefits or programs, but at the same time balance the budget. The Coalition was founded on the premise that when faced this dilemma, too few legislators summon the courage to make the difficult decisions necessary to balance the budget. As a result, the Coalition's goal is to try to get politicians to change direction through lobbying legislators and educating constituents. The Concord Coalition remains unwavering in its belief that though deficits may be good short-term politics, they are bad long-term fiscal policy. Washington policymakers, the Concord Coalition argues, "should focus on regaining budget surpluses as soon as is practicable."

The Concord Coalition has released annual deficit reduction scores for members of Congress since 1995. The Coalition's so-called "Fiscal Responsibility Scorecard" gives each legislator a score between 0 and 100. Votes deemed to have a significant impact on deficit reduction were assigned various weights according to their relative importance. Concord calculated the raw scores by adding the weights of a legislator's "fiscally responsible" votes and dividing this figure by the total weighted value of the votes cast by that legislator. Votes for which the legislator did not vote are excluded. The votes selected for the Concord Coalition's rating were chosen because they:

1) Reduced the deficit/protected the surplus.
2) Supported actions that address long-term generational pressures on the federal budget.
3) Kept the budget enforcement procedures strong.
4) Opposed enactment of new permanent claims on the federal budget that would be difficult to finance in the future.
5) Reduced or eliminated unnecessary or wasteful programs.

The fact that the Concord Coalition considers the tax side of the budget to be equal to the spending side of the budget in its political and economic importance is a beneficial attribute of the Concord Coalition's scores–the Concord Coalition measures a legislator's tendency to support deficit reduction in terms of both taxing and spending. To the Concord Coalition, "fiscal responsibility" is voting in favor of reduced spending or increased taxes and voting against increased spending or reduced taxes. Thus, the Concord Coalition's congressional vote scores can be seen as a means of measuring individual representatives and senators wiliness to support the principles of balancing the budget from both the revenue side of the budget as well as the expenditure side of the budget.

Officially, the Concord Coalition is a nonpartisan entity, but it is possible that there may be partisan patterns as to which legislators are rated highly by the organization.   Partisanship has increasingly been found to influence the direction of congressional roll call votes and ideologically the parties have polarized since the mid-1970s.[31] Partisanship, however, is not an infallible predictor. Roll calls often split one or both of the parties. These splits are due at least in part due to the fact that legislators have parochial interests. Given the nature of a members' support, it can be to the benefit of individual members of Congress to go out of their way to protect the interests and preferences of his or her partisan electoral coalition. For Republicans in Congress, for instance, this may lead them to support tax cuts even if it is seems to contradict district opinion; for Democrats this may put pressure on them to increase spending totals beyond that which is favored by their constituency as a whole.

Both parties can claim legitimate ideological grounds for supporting balancing the budget. Democrats may see attempts to cut taxes and move the budget toward deficits as a long-term means to reduce spending benefitting Democratic constituencies and thus may be more favorable toward balanced budget policies than the Republicans. Republicans, on the other hand, may see reducing the national debt as a means to reduce taxes in the long run, thus enticing them to support balancing the budget. Economic issues such as measures to balance the budget, therefore, may now be viewed as a defining ideological difference between the parties.

Comparing the mean annual Concord Coalition vote scores of the parties, Democrats and Republicans do indeed have notably different ratings in both houses of Congress (see Table 5.6). An interesting characteristic of the effect of partisanship on the Concord Coalition vote

Table 5.6
Mean Annual Concord Coalition Vote Scores by Party

| | House | | Senate | |
	Democrats	Republicans	Democrats	Republicans
Year				
1995	36.00	**51.51*****	42.34	**48.74*****
1996	**49.03**	45.82**	46.38	**56.81*****
1997	53.92	**58.78*****	49.69	**61.20*****
1998	**43.05**	29.20***	43.98	**46.64**
1999	**40.74**	30.10***	**33.04**	24.06**
2000	**34.77**	33.82	**33.98**	27.64**

***$p < .001$; **$p < .01$; *$p < .05$
Party with highest annual mean in **bold**

scores, however, is that even though party is a statistically significant predictor ($p < .01$) of Concord Coalition vote scores for five of the six years between 1995-2000, the direction of partisan influences in not consistent. That is, for some years being a Republican has a positive effect on scores by the Concord Coalition, in other years there is a positive relationship being a Democrat. This suggests that both Democrats and Republicans can occasionally make the claim of being the party of fiscal responsibility.

Yet, importantly, a distinguishable pattern can be seen. In the House, in 1995 and 1997 the Republicans had higher mean Concord Coalition vote scores and in 1996 and from 1998-2000 the Democrats did. In the Senate, the Republicans had higher scores from 1995-1998 and the Democrats in 1999 and 2000. Thus, since the Concord Coalition begun giving scores to members of Congress in 1995 there has been a shift from the Republicans getting overall higher scores to the Democrats being more supportive of the organization's goals. The dramatic change in the party's Concord Coalition vote scores can be especially seen in the House. In 1995, the Republicans had an average score of over 51 and the Democrats of 36. By 1998, however, the Republicans' mean score had declined to 29 and the Democrats' had increased to 43. Unquestionably an important shift occurred.

It has been found that a liberal/conservative ordering of members of Congress is a predominant feature of nearly all roll call voting.[32] The Concord Coalition's congressional roll call vote ratings, however, do not fit nicely on the standard left-right political spectrum, suggesting that the political dynamics of deficit reduction are different from those of other issues. The fact that the Concord Coalition may be an atypical interest group that cannot be distinguished by where the group stands on the ideological spectrum can also be seen by looking at the individual members of the House and Senate who received the highest annual "Fiscal Responsibility" scores. As can be seen from Table 5.7, the highest scores given to House members include legislators from across the political spectrum. In 2000, for example, the top five Concord Coalition scores in the House included a representative who would probably be regarded by most congressional observers as a relatively liberal Democrat (Lloyd Doggett), a conservative Democrat (Charles Stenholm), and three conservative Republicans (Mark Sanford, Tom Coburn and Ed Royce). While in 1995 Republican representatives had the five highest scores, in 1999 Democratic representatives had the five highest scores.

The fact that neither party dominates the Concord Coalition's list of high scores can also be seen in the organization's Senate ratings. In every year that the Concord Coalition published its ratings from 1995-2000 neither party had more than three of the highest five scores. The senators who received the highest annual rating by the Concord Coalition is truly a heterogeneous group from across the political spectrum; those who received the highest annual score include Democrats Russ Feingold, Charles Robb, and Herb Kohl, and Republicans Daniel Coats and Hank Brown.

From the New Deal era to election of Ronald Reagan as president, it was widely held that Republicans put a higher premium on balancing the budget than Democrats. To be "conservative" on fiscal policy meant that your were averse to deficits. Since 1980, however, fiscal policy has bifurcated. Though conservatives and Republicans still tend to support budgetary balance in the abstract, they apparently are less willing than previously to support the concept when presented with the specifics. Democrats and liberals, on the other hand, increasingly support deficit reduction–at least when it is defined in their terms.[33]

One possible explanation for the Democrats replacing Republicans in recent years as being more likely to support deficit reduction has to due with the arrival of the federal budget surplus and the parties budgetary priorities. After the 1994 elections in which the

Table 5.7
Concord Coalition's Top Five Annual
"Fiscal Responsibility" Scores

House:

2000	*1999*	*1998*
Doggett (D-TX)	Doggett (D-TX)	Sanford (R-SC)
Sanford (R-SC)	Luther (D-MN)	Skaggs (D-CO)
Coburn (R-OK)	Meehan (D-MA)	Barrett (D-WI)
Royce (R-CA)	Barrett (D-WI)	Kind (D-WI)
Stenholm (D-TX)	Minge (D-MN)	Castle (R-DE)

1997	*1996*	*1995*
Meehan (D-MA)	Morella (R-MD)	Klug (R-WI)
Barrett (D-WI)	Porter (R-IL)	Duncan (R-TN)
Campbell (R-CA)	Roukema (R-NJ)	Upton (R-MI)
Minge (D-MN)	Campbell (R-CA)	Blute (R-MA)
Davis (R-FL)	Meehan (D-MA)	Morella (R-MD)

Senate:

2000	*1999*	*1998*
Feingold (D-WI)	Feingold (D-WI)	Coats (R-IN)
Voinovich (R-OH)	Voinovich (R-OH)	Feingold (D-WI)
McCain (R-AZ)	Graham (D-FL)	Moynihan(D-NY)
Kerrey (D-NB)	McCain (R-AZ)	Robb (D-VA)
Bryan (D-NV)	Fitzgerald (R-IL)	Grams (R-MN)

1997	*1996*	*1995*
Robb (D-VA)	Kohl (D-WI)	Brown (R-CO)
Kohl (D-WI)	Brown (R-CO)	Kerrey (D-NB)
Grassley (R-IA)	Cohen (R-ME)	Nunn (D-GA)
McCain (R-AZ)	Jeffords (R-VT)	Robb (D-VA)
Nickles (R-OK)	Nunn (D-GA)	Snowe (R-ME)

Republicans took control of Congress, annual deficits were still relatively high. Thus, the Republicans, even though they publicly supported significant tax cuts, made cutting domestic spending a higher legislative priority. With a Democrat in the White House, congressional Republicans may have decided they would be more successful passing legislation that reduced spending than enacting tax cuts. With the advent of federal budget surpluses in 1998, however, the Republicans made a more concentrated effort to reduce taxes and the Democrats, playing defensive, voted against the tax cuts arguing that the surplus would be better used for domestic programs and reducing the national debt. Thus, immediately after the Republicans took control of Congress they had higher Concord Coalition vote scores because they controlled the legislative agenda and supported a number of measures to reduce federal spending that Democrats opposed. By 1998, however, the Republicans moved toward making tax cuts a greater priority, lowering their scores, while Democrats' opposition of tax cuts garnered them higher "fiscal responsibility" scores.

To a large degree, therefore, which party is seen to be a better advocate of balanced budget policies has to do with whether it is a spending or taxing issue that is being debated. The Republicans are going to be seen as the better advocates of the balanced budget when it comes to attempts to keep spending down, but the Democrats are going to better seen as better defenders of balanced budget priorities when it comes to tax legislation. Given the major priority tax reduction has been has given in the George W. Bush administration, including the significant tax cuts in the 2001 Budget Reconciliation Bill–a measure the Concord Coalition strongly opposed because it eliminated much of the projected federal surpluses over the next decade–it may be safe to predict that the Democrats can be expected to receive higher vote scores by the Concord Coalition throughout the George W. Bush presidency.

Thus, at least in recent years, a strong argument can be made that the Democratic party has done a better job of keeping budget deficit totals down than the Republican party. This argument is reinforced if we look at deficit and surplus totals by presidential administration. An analysis of deficit and surplus totals since the Kennedy administration shows that deficits have tended to be significantly higher under Republican administrations (see Table 5.8). From 1962-2003, the average deficit of budgets enacted with a Democrat as president was $12.3 billion (the mean annual deficits of budgets enacted by Kennedy was $6.0 billion, Johnson $7.2 billion, Carter $63.3 billion, and the average annual budget surplus of budgets passed during the Clinton administration was $7.6 billion) and

Table 5.8
Deficits and Surpluses by Party Controlling the White House

Year	Surplus or Deficit (-)	As % of GDP	President*	Party	Divided Govt.
1962	-7	-1.3	Kennedy	D	No
1963	-5	-0.8	Kennedy	D	No
1964	-6	-0.9	Kennedy	D	No
1965	-1	-0.2	Johnson	D	No
1966	-4	-0.5	Johnson	D	No
1967	-9	-1.1	Johnson	D	No
1968	-25	-2.9	Johnson	D	No
1969	3	0.3	Johnson	D	No
1970	-3	-0.3	Nixon	R	Yes
1971	-23	-2.1	Nixon	R	Yes
1972	-23	-2.0	Nixon	R	Yes
1973	-15	-1.1	Nixon	R	Yes
1974	-6	-0.4	Nixon	R	Yes
1975	-53	-3.4	Ford	R	Yes
1976	-74	-4.2	Ford	R	Yes
1977	-54	-2.7	Ford	R	Yes
1978	-59	-2.7	Carter	D	No
1979	-41	-1.6	Carter	D	No
1980	-74	-2.7	Carter	D	No
1981	-79	-2.6	Carter	D	No
1982	-128	-4.0	Reagan	R	Yes
1983	-208	-6.0	Reagan	R	Yes
1984	-185	-4.8	Reagan	R	Yes
1985	-212	-5.1	Reagan	R	Yes
1986	-221	-5.0	Reagan	R	Yes
1987	-150	-3.2	Reagan	R	Yes
1988	-155	-3.1	Reagan	R	Yes
1989	-153	-2.8	Reagan	R	Yes
1990	-221	-3.9	Bush	R	Yes
1991	-269	-4.5	Bush	R	Yes
1992	-290	-4.7	Bush	R	Yes
1993	-255	-3.9	Bush	R	Yes

Table 5.8 (Continued)

Year	Surplus or Deficit (-)	As % of GDP	President*	Party	Divided Govt.
1994	-203	-2.9	Clinton	D	No
1995	-164	-2.2	Clinton	D	No
1996	-108	-1.4	Clinton	D	Yes
1997	-22	-0.3	Clinton	D	Yes
1998	69	0.8	Clinton	D	Yes
1999	126	1.4	Clinton	D	Yes
2000	236	2.4	Clinton	D	Yes
2001	127	1.3	Clinton	D	Yes
2002	-158	-1.5	Bush	R	No^
2003	-375	-3.4	Bush	R	Yes

* = The president who was in office when the fiscal year budget was enacted by Congress (the previous year), not who was president that year
^ = Republicans controlled House and Senate at time 2002 fiscal budget was passed
Surplus and Deficit figures in billions of dollars
Source: Congressional Budget Office

the average deficit of budgets initiated by Republican presidents was $146.9 billion (with average annual budget deficits of $14.0 billion of those budgets passed during the Nixon administration, $60.3 billion during the Ford administration, $176.5 billion during the Reagan administration, $258.8 billion during the elder George Bush presidency, and $266.5 billion during the first two years of the George W. Bush administration), a statistically significant difference ($p < .001$) (see Table 5.9). The budget deficits enacted under Republican presidents were on average more than 11 times greater than those produced under Democratic presidents. As a percentage of the Gross Domestic Product (GDP), the difference between deficits produced by Democratic and Republican presidents was not quite as dramatic, but was also statistically significant ($p < .001$): the average deficit of a budget instituted under Democratic presidencies was 0.89 percent of the GDP while deficits enacted under Republican presidencies averaged 3.28 percent of the GDP.

Table 5.9
Deficits by Presidential Party

	Democratic President	Republican President
Average Deficit (billions)	12.3	146.9***
Average Deficit as % of GDP	0.89	3.28***

***p < .001

These figures lend support to Democratic arguments that they have been better guardians of balancing the budget, at least from the White House.

Presidents, of course, do not produce budgets in a vacuum. Congress, after all, has the final say in whether or not a budget is eventually enacted and as a result the White House must consider potential congressional support when constructing budgets. Especially important in this regard is weather or not the president's party has a majority in the House and the Senate, which has been an increasingly rare occurrence since the 1950s.

Partisanship in Congress may be reinforced by the prevalence of divided government. Divided government creates incentives for Congress to use divisive public policy debates on so-called "wedge issues" in order to damage the opposing party in future elections.[34] Another possible consequence of divided government is that if the president and Congress cannot reach agreement, then inflows and outflows will be out of balance. Depending on factors such as the state of the economy, either deficits or surpluses are possible under a divided government that can't reach a budgetary consensus.[35]

The budgetary polarization that occurs in periods of divided government may make balancing the budget more problematic. Since the Kennedy administration that has arguably been the case. The average budget deficit under divided governments from 1962-2003 was $98.0 billion (2.46 percent of the GDP) while the average budget deficits under unified governments was only $55.5 billion (1.57 percent of the GDP) (see Table 5.10). Though not statistically significant, budget deficits since 1962 have thus on average been more than 75 percent higher in periods of divided government.

Table 5.10
Deficits by Type of Government

	Divided Government	Unified Government
Average Deficit (billions)	98.0	55.5
Average Deficit as % of GDP	2.46	1.57

A Too Partisan Budget Process?

Decisions regarding congressional budget priorities are partially the result of constituency influences. As the constituencies electing Democrats and Republicans to Congress have become more distinct, the partisanship of the congressional budget process has increased. Political parties have never been further apart on budget priorities than they are today. As American government has grown, the federal budget process has become less stable and consensual.[37] As a result, the budgetary conflict in today in Congress is historically unprecedented. Republicans strong support for reducing taxes and the Democrats hostility toward the concept can be viewed as a consequence of the nature of congressional representation. The differences in the tax policy orientations of the parties are simply a result of members trying to represent the voters who have elected them to Congress, which are increasingly becoming more disparate.

Given the acute partisan divide on budgetary issues, it can be argued that congressional budgeting has become too partisan, creating an environment not conducive toward the compromises necessary for agreement. Extreme partisanship can polarize the budget process; yet, at the same time, it can be argued that the parties are too weak because they largely fail to act as mechanisms for achieving collective responsibility. Some form of collective responsibility is essential in producing a budget accountable to the people.

Party is an organizing mechanism of Congress that it cannot do without. Members of Congress are elected under a variety of constituencies. The mix within congressional parties is a product of the mix within the nation's constituencies. The net result of this diversity is that members see the world in different ways, stress different values, and pursue different budgetary objectives. A vast amount of disagreement inevitably lurks behind each party's label. The parties in Congress are weak because each individual member's career comes first, power within the body is fragmented, the intricacies of the legislative process make it difficult for the parties to function smoothly and effectively, and because the congressional party is a microcosm of the party in the electorate, beset by the same internal conflicts.[37]

Party responsibility provides party members with a personal stake in their collective performance. Parties provide the glue to hold together the disparate parts of a fragmented Congress. Parties unite us as few other institutions do and permit Congress to rally around a common standard. The parties draw together ideologically diverse elements to the benefit of the institution of Congress as a whole by converting the numerous social and economic groups in this nation into some patterns of choice that are more comprehensible.[38] The parties have the potential of being a strong mechanism for measuring Congress' collective performance. As the election results of 1994 show, if the voters are unhappy with the direction of Congress as an institution, they can take action against the party in power.

The parties have an important role in the creation of the budget and the presentation of what the budget entails to the American people. Political parties are needed to get a budget through Congress that makes sense from a macrobudget viewpoint. Parties are also needed to provide a sense of collective responsibility for the consequences of what is in the budget. Yet, at the same time, it is possible that extreme partisanship could polarize the congressional budget process.[39] The parties have the potential of being a destructive force in congressional budgeting if partisanship and political maneuvering dominate the process. The task for Congress, therefore, is to use partisanship in a manner constructive to the formation of a national budget. Given the checks and balances of the American political system, compromise is a necessary element of the congressional budget process. Partisanship is thereby a necessary component in the congressional budget process, but a component that must conduct itself within the boundaries of the American political system. The will and ability of members of Congress to compromise political goals for what is good for the country is a necessary ingredient in the budget process.

Endnotes

1. E.E. Schattschneider, *The Semisovereign People* (New York: Holt, Rinehart and Winston, 1960), p. 68.

2. Tsai-Tsu Su, Mark Kamlet, and David Mowery, "Modeling U.S. Budgetary and Fiscal Policy Outcomes: A Disaggregated Systemwide Perspective," *American Journal of Political Science* 37 (1993): 213-245.

3. Louis Hartz, *The Liberal Tradition in America* (New York: Harcourt, Brace and World, Inc., 1955).

4. Steven Koven, *Ideological Budgeting* (New York: Praeger, 1988), pp. 55-56.

5. Ibid., pp. 127-128.

6. Philip Converse, "The Stability of Belief Elements Over Time," *Ideology and Discontent*, David Apter, ed. (New York: Free Press, 1964) and Eric Smith, *The Unchanging American Voter* (Berkeley: University of California Press, 1989).

7. Frank Sorauf and Paul Allen Beck, *Party Politics in America*, 6th ed. (Glenview, IL: Scott, Foresman and Company, 1988), p. 396.

8. Ibid., p. 423.

9. William Keefe, *Parties, Politics, and Public Policy in America*, 6th ed. (Washington, D.C.: CQ Press, 1991), p. 37.

10. Sorauf and Beck, p. 421 and Keefe, p. 254.

11. Ibid., p. 421.

12. David Rhode, "Electoral Forces, Political Agendas, and Partisanship in the House and Senate," *The Postreform Congress*, Rodger Davidson ed., pp. 27-47 (New York: St. Martin's Press, 1992), p. 27.

13. Richard Fenno, *The Power of the Purse* (Boston: Little, Brown and Company, 1966), p. 245.

14. Ibid., p. 233.

15. Steven Schier, *A Decade of Deficits* (Albany: SUNY Press, 1992), p. 26.

16. Irene Rubin, *Balancing the Federal Budget* (New York: Chatham House, 2003), p. 34.

17. John Cranford, *Budgeting for America* (Washington, D.C.: CQ Press, 1989), p. 141.

18. Joseph White and Aaron Wildavsky, *The Deficit and the Public Interest* (Berkeley: University of California Press, 1989), p. 412.

19. Guy Peters, *The Politics of Taxation* (Cambridge, MA: Blackwell, 1991), pp. 118-123.

20. John Ellwood, "Budget Reform and Interchamber Relations," *Congressional Budgeting*, W. Thomas Wander, F. Ted Herbert and Gary Copeland eds., pp. 100-132 (Baltimore: John Hopkins Press, 1984).

21. The Rice Index of Cohesion is measured by subtracting the percentage against a bill (the budget resolutions in this case) from the percentage for the bill. The Rice index is then expressed as the absolute difference between the two percentage figures. According to *Legislative Roll-Call Analysis* by Lee Anderson, Meredith Watts, and Allen Wilcox (Evanston: Northwestern University Press, 1966) this measure defines "cohesion as the extent to which the distribution of votes on a legislative roll call deviates from the distribution that would be expected if all influences operated in a random fashion" (p. 32).

22. Lance Leloup, *The Fiscal Congress* (Westport, CT: Greenwood Press, 1980), p. 103.

23. Dennis Ippolito, *Congressional Spending* (Ithaca: Cornell University Press, 1981), pp. 106-115.

24. Ellwood (1984)

25. Benjamin I. Page, Robert Y. Shapiro, Paul W. Gronke and Robert W. Rosenberg, "Constituency, Party, and Representation in Congress" *Public Opinion Quarterly* 48 (1984): 741-756; Morris Fiorina, *Representatives, Roll Calls, and Constituencies* (Lexington, MA: Lexington Books, 1974); W. Wayne Shannon, *Party, Constituency and Congressional Voting* (Baton Rouge: LSU Press, 1968).

26. David Brady, *Congressional Voting in a Partisan Era* (Lawrence: University of Kansas Press, 1973).

27. Jeffrey M. Stonecash, *Class and Party in American Politics* (Boulder, CO: Westview Press, 2000).

28. Ibid.

29. Fiorina (1974).

30. Allen Schick, *The Capacity to Budget* (Washington, DC: The Urban Institute, 1990).

31. Concord Coalition, "Introduction to the Concord Coalition's Fiscal Responsibility Scorecard" http://www.concordcoalition.org July 2, 2001.

32. Keith T. Poole and Howard Rosenthal, *Congress: A Political-Economic History of Roll Call Voting* (New York: Oxford University Press, 1997).

33. Ibid.

34. Andrew J. Taylor, "The Ideological Roots of Deficit Reduction Policy," *The Review of Policy Research* 19 (2002): 11-29.

35. Melody Rose, "Divided Government and the Rise of Social Regulation" *Policy Studies Journal* 29 (2001): 611-626.

36. Morris Fiorina, *Divided Government*, 2nd ed., (Boston: Allyn and Bacon, 1996).

37. Dennis Ippolito, *Why Budgets Matter: Budget Policy and American Politics* (University Park: Pennsylvania State University Press, 2003).

38. Keefe (1991), pp. 271-273.

39. Larry Sabato, *The Party's Just Begun* (Glenview, IL: Scott, Forseman and Company, 1988).

40. Koven (1988), pp. 127-28.

Chapter 6

Congressional Budgeting and Public Opinion

Public Opinion as a Determinant of Budget Priorities

Why should Members of Congress worry about public opinion? Public opinion is important because it moves election outcomes, and through them public policy. Policy mood has much in common with popular beliefs about eras and there is a strong correlation between policy mood and congressional elections.[1]

Yet, even if Congress wants to follow public opinion, it may not be able to do. Following the dictates of pubic opinion is not a cut-and-dry process. It is often difficult to tell what public opinion is, and a government that takes public opinion into account tends to be cross-pressured by contradictory desires.[2] This is especially the case in terms of budgeting; should the government follow the citizens' desire for lower taxes, or should it follow the citizens' desire for lower deficits? Since there is a strong correlation between public mood on the issues and government action, the power over the budget is potentially in the hands of the citizenry. If the people are divided, the task then belongs to members of Congress to produce a budget that serves both long-term and short-term economic goals and can be accepted by most Americans.

While the electoral sanction may be central to democratic governance, it has been argued that congressional incumbents have such advantages that the electorate does not have a meaningful say in who does and does not belong in office.[3]   If members of Congress do not fear electoral retribution, then its members may be more likely to make budgetary votes without considering public opinion. Individual members of Congress may be able to avoid being tarnished by negative impressions of the institution as a whole. Citizens' attitudes toward Congress correspond with veto overrides, intra-Congress conflict and the passage of major bills.[4] There are discrepancies between what people expect Congress to be like and what they perceive it actually is like that negatively affect evaluations of Congress.[5] Yet, while the standing of Congress as an institution is low, the approval ratings of individual members is not.[6]

Public opinion, however, has been found to have a major impact on voting in congressional elections even when congressional actions seem to contradict public opinion. After the 1990 Budget was completed that raised income taxes and cut entitlements spending, public opinion polls showed that the public was overwhelmingly against the measure. Yet the measure was still passed just prior to the November elections. It was found that members of Congress were sensitive to the electoral implications of the 1990 Budget, but the bill passed because "few members faced opponents who posed a serious electoral threat; most were in a position to absorb the anticipated political damage without risking their careers."[7] In fact, electoral risk was by far the best predictor of weather or not a member would vote against the 1990 Budget; the budget passed because few perceived themselves to be at electoral risk for the upcoming elections. Stronger support in one's constituency made it easier to vote for an unpopular bill. But in both the House and the Senate, voting for the deficit reduction bill significantly reduced an incumbent's vote. Incumbents tried to avoid individual responsibility for a bill when it may have cost them reelection.

Public opinion may shape the collective behavior of Congress, but at the same time its influence on substantive policy decisions of individual members has been found to be modest. In one study, there was little evidence that public opinion exerted a direct influence on the positions taken by individual legislators. In fact, members were found to be suspicious of opinion polls, and most claimed public opinion only slightly influenced them. On the other hand, Congressional leaders have the ability during certain circumstances to bring the public around to adopting their preferred policies.[8] Thus, Congress might not be following public opinion but actually creating it.

Public Opinion and Deficits

Although the public clearly disapproves of deficits, it also objects to doing anything conclusive and drastic about them–a state of opinion reflected in the actions of Congress. In fact, the movement of taxing and spending may be said to be reasonably in accord with the preferences of the mass public. The crisis of budget politics today is not a failure to bring the general interest into the political debate–it is just the opposite. There is a conflict between what the public says it wants (i.e., a balanced budget) and how it votes (i.e., penalizing those who support raising taxes). The policy instructions from the public sphere, therefore, contradict the instructions legislators receive directly from their constituents.[9]

Deficits are in part the result of the fact that members of Congress listen to their constituents. Polling data suggest that the public is ambivalent about deficit reduction measures. While a large majority of citizens favor a balanced budget, they do not want higher taxes and they do not want to cut spending for most programs.[10] In one public opinion poll, the public was divided when asked if they were personally willing to make sacrifices, such as paying higher taxes and receiving fewer benefits, to reduce the federal budget deficit. Just over half (51 percent) indicated they were willing to make sacrifices, and 45 percent said they were not.[11] Part of the public's reluctance to pay new taxes may stem from the fact that, though it says it wants a balanced budget, reducing the deficit is not that high of a priority, relatively speaking. When asked what they believe is the most important problem facing this country today, the deficit came in fifth, behind health care, the economy in general, unemployment, and crime.[12]

The fact that deficit reduction might not be that high of a priority with the public can also be seen by the public opinion data presented in Table 6.1. Though the public favors a balanced budget amendment in the abstract, most (Republicans as well as Democrats) oppose such an amendment if it means cuts in Social Security and a substantial share of the population preferred to cut taxes over balancing the budget.

The public's lack of concern toward the nation running in the red can be seen in their political responses. President Ronald Reagan is the classic example of the fact that voters do not punish politicians for large deficits. In an April, 1984 poll, voters were asked, "Regardless of your own political views, what would you give as the best reason for voting against President Reagan?" The deficit ranked ninth with four percent, far behind foreign policy (21 percent) and fairness (18 percent).[13] Thus,

Table 6.1
Opinions on Balanced Budget

	Republicans	Independents	Democrats
Say they would prefer:			
Balancing the budget over cutting taxes	59%	59%	51%
Cutting taxes over balancing the budget	37%	37%	45%
Favor a balanced budget amendment to the Constitution	82%	79%	79%
Oppose	11%	12%	13%
Favor a balanced budget amendment even if it means cuts in Social Security	40%	32%	25%
Oppose	56%	63%	72%

Source: New York Time/CBS News Poll, based on interviews with 1,190 adults conducted nationwide February 22-25, 1995. Those with no opinion not shown.

even though deficits skyrocketed during his administration, Reagan was able to win reelection in a landslide. At the same time over 95 percent of the members of Congress who cooperated with Reagan in producing these deficits were reelected between 1982 and 1988.[14] Voters have simply not retaliated against politicians who have produced deficits. Thus, the electorate must share the blame for the deficits Congress has been producing. Many citizens are aware of this problem. A majority of the public (60 percent) say that the American people themselves are just as much to blame as Congress for the current budget deficit. When asked if the budget deficit is "mostly because Congress is unwilling to do the right thing" or "because the American people are unwilling to make the necessary sacrifices,"five percent said the latter, 37 percent the former, and 55 percent both.[15]

Table 6.2
Framing the Question: Budget Cuts

Question 1: Do you favor or oppose the proposal for a constitutional amendment to require a balanced Federal budget by the year 2002 and every year after that?

Favor	70%
Oppose	18%
Don't know/refused	12%

Question 2: Do you favor or oppose the proposal for a constitutional amendment to require a balanced budget that cuts Government spending on Medicare by 20 percent over the next seven years?

Favor	31%
Oppose	58%
Don't know/refused	11%

Question 3: Actually, so much money is being spent on Medicare that even a $350 billion cut in projected spending would still be a 50 percent increase over today's spending levels. Now what would you tell your member of Congress to do?

Don't cut from Medicare; find cuts elsewhere	36%
Let spending on Medicare grow to keep pace with inflation and the growing number of elderly	25%
Keep the growth of Medicare to 50% increase over seven years	16%
Cut Medicare spending	13%
Don't know/refused	10%

Source: *New York Times*, June 15, 1995, p. A1.

Americans tend to have contradictory opinions in regards to deficits and balancing the budget. The contradictory wants of the American public in terms of budget cuts can be seen in Table 6.2, which displays how much the phrasing of a question affects what the public says it wants when it comes to budgeting and proposed cuts in Medicare spending. Since Americans tend to invest only brief attention to budgetary issues, and tend to make up their minds on the basis of key words and phrases that they hear, the manner in which a proposal is framed can determine its success in a Congress that is always acutely aware of public opinion.

These contradictory signals on budget priorities make life difficult for members of Congress. The problems that federal officials face when budgeting are in part a result of the inconsistencies of what the public says it wants. Although the public clearly disapproves of deficits, it also objected to doing anything conclusive and drastic about them–a state of opinion reflected in the actions of the federal government. Polls showed that while the federal government was producing large deficits most respondents voiced a concern about the deficit but at the same time were reluctant to pay higher taxes and were opposed to suggested program cuts.[16] A 1977 poll, for example, showed that there was strong support for cutting income taxes even if that meant a larger budget deficit (see Figure 6.1). The large deficits that plagued the federal government may therefore be said to be reasonably in accord with the preferences of the mass public.[17] Thus, deficits were in part the result of the fact the members of Congress (as well as the White House) listened to their constituents.

The budgetary political battles of the early 1980s taught Republicans that opposition to taxes was good politics, but attacking popular domestic programs was not. Budget action faithful to the electoral stances guaranteed large deficits.[18] The large deficits of the 1980s and early 1990s were the result of conflicting party preferences under divided government.[19]

Thus, the deficits of the past were thus in part the result of the fact that members of Congress listen to their constituents. The American public was ambivalent about deficit reduction measures. The public was divided when asked if they were personally willing to make sacrifices, such as paying higher taxes and receiving fewer benefits, to reduce the federal budget deficit. While a large majority of citizens favored a balanced budget in the abstract, they did not want higher taxes and they did not want to cut spending for most programs.[20]

Figure 6.1
Public Opinion on Taxes and the Deficit–1977

"Are you in favor of a cut in federal income taxes, or not?"

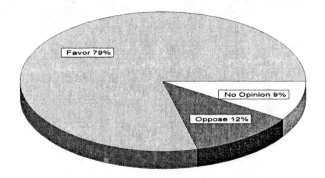

Asked of those who favored a tax cut: "Would you still favor a cut in federal income taxes even if that meant a larger government deficit?"

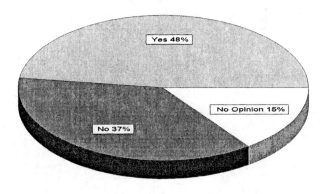

Source: Gallup Poll (Survey # 966-K) conducted January 14-17, 1977.
Margin of error +/- 3 points.

Public Opinion and the Surpluses of 1998-2001

The federal government found itself unable to raise enough revenues to meet spending demands throughout the 1970s, 1980s, and most of the 1990s, yet by 2000 the federal governments found itself producing record surpluses. The ability of the federal government to produce surpluses from 1998-2001 was related to changes in public opinion. To some degree, the contradictions of citizen demands were mitigated. The public's perception of taxing and spending priorities became more supportive of deficit and debt reduction. Congress was able to produce budgetary surplus mainly because of an unexpected windfall of revenues. But a changed climate in public opinion also aided Congress in this endeavor. This is especially true when it came to public opinion on taxation.

Tax cuts have a generic appeal to Americans. When the public is asked if they favor a "cut in federal income taxes," the responses are overwhelmingly positive. Americans also consistently say that they pay too much in federal income taxes.[21] The popularity of tax cuts, however, is significantly different when it is placed in context against other proposals (see Table 6.3). When Americans were asked in 1999 if they preferred increased spending in general or tax cuts, the response was overwhelmingly (74%) in favor of tax cuts. When in competition with funding popular programs, however, tax cuts lose much of their appeal. Only 36% of Americans said that they would prefer cutting taxes as opposed to funding new retirement savings accounts and increasing spending on education, defense, Medicare and other programs.

Part of the lack of support for tax cuts may be derived from the fact that Americans tend to believe that upper-income people are paying too little in federal taxes compared to lower- and middle-income people. While 51% of Americans believed that lower-income people paid "too much" in federal taxes and 59% believed the same of middle-income people, only 10% said that upper-income people paid "too much" in federal taxes. On the other hand, nearly two-thirds of those polled responded that upper-income people contributed "too little" in income taxes (see Table 6.4).

The fact that most Americans do not believe that upper-income people are paying their "fair share" in taxes has important consequences for the federal government's ability to balance the budget. Though surveys have revealed that substantial income redistribution has never been popular in the United States, Americans have always strongly supported a progressive income tax.[22] And since an increase in the

Table 6.3
Priority of Tax Cuts

"As you may know, the federal government is currently running a budget surplus, meaning it is taking in more money than it spends. President Clinton and Republicans in Congress agree most of the surplus money should be used for Social Security, but they disagree over what to do with the rest. How would you prefer to see the rest of the budget surplus used?"

Option 1:

To increase spending on other government programs	21%
To cut taxes	74%
Neither/Other	1%

Option 2:

To fund new retirement savings accounts, as well as increase spending on education, defense, Medicare and other programs	59%
To cut taxes	36%
Neither/Other	5%

Source: Gallup Poll of 505 (option 1) and 516 (option 2) adults nationwide June 4-5, 1999. Margin of error +/-5 percentage points.

Table 6.4
"Fair Share" of Taxes by Income Group

"As I read off some different groups, please tell me if you think they are paying their fair share in federal taxes, paying too much, or paying too little?"

	Fair Share	Too Much	Too Little	No Opinion
"Lower-income people"	34%	51%	11%	4%
"Middle-income people"	35%	59%	4%	2%
"Upper-income people"	19%	10%	66%	5%

Source: Gallup Poll of 1,055 adults nationwide April 6-7, 1999. Margin of error +/-3 percentage points.

progressivity of the income tax can result in significantly higher tax revenues, increasing tax rates on the wealthy is potentially a politically acceptable means of raising more revenue. The success of the progressive tax increases of the 1993 Budget Reconciliation Bill at reducing the federal deficit indicates that a more progressive income tax may be a solution to eliminating deficits.

The fact that the 1993 Budget's tax increases were on upper-incomes marked a return to traditional Democratic-style budgets of the post-New Deal era. Though the two new tax brackets that were created (36% and 39.6%) were much smaller than the highest tax brackets of the previous Democratic presidencies since the New Deal, the return to a more progressive income tax was a significant shift from the tax policies of Ronald Reagan and George Bush. After 1992, the last year the highest income tax rate was 31%, the federal government gained substantially more revenue from those with higher incomes. Because of the widened income gap between low and high earners, the federal government took in much more revenue than it would have without the 1993 tax increases.[23] The individual income taxes received by the federal government from those making over $100,000 increased over 76 percent in the four years after the tax provisions of the 1993 Budget became law.

Table 6.5
Surplus Priorities

"Given the budget surplus, what priority should these proposals be given?"

	Top	*Low/None*
Strengthen Social Security	32%	13%
Reduce National Debt	31%	18%
Strengthen Medicare	28%	15%
Increase Education Funding	25%	23%
Cut Income Taxes	22%	34%
Child Care Tax Credits	20%	35%
Tax Credits to Reduce Pollution	15%	42%
Increase Spending on Highways	11%	58%

Source: Gallup Poll of 1,013 adults nationwide August 17-18, 1999. Margin of error +/-3 percentage points.

Millionaires contributed more than twice as much to the Federal Treasury in 1996 than they did in 1992, the year prior the passage of the 1993 Budget Reconciliation Bill. Thus, the progressive nature of the tax increases has played a significant role in the reduction of the deficit. The government taxed the economic winners of the 1990s, redistributing income while boosting its revenues.[24]

Since the increase in the federal government's revenues were disproportionately from the wealthy after the top income tax rates were raised in 1993, the fact that the public did not tend to support reducing taxes for those with upper-incomes increased the likelihood of surpluses. Thus, public opinion in regards to taxing the wealthy during the later stages of the Clinton administration may have facilitated the ability of the federal government to produce balanced budgets.

In regards to the conflict between the Republican Congress and the Democratic White House over what to do with the budget surplus, from a public opinion perspective it seemed as though President Clinton may have had the upper hand. Public opinion in 1999 and 2000 was

Figure 6.2
Opinions on Surplus

"As you may know, the federal government is running a budget surplus this year. In your opinion, which one of the following should be done with the money from the surplus?"

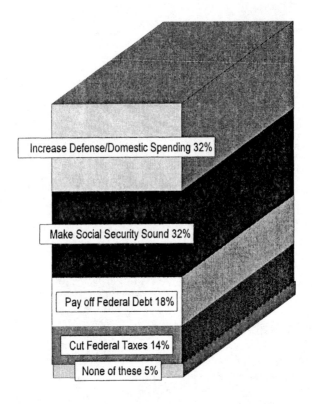

Increase Defense/Domestic Spending 32%

Make Social Security Sound 32%

Pay off Federal Debt 18%

Cut Federal Taxes 14%

None of these 5%

Source: Bloomsberg News Poll 0f 1,208 adults nationwide conducted by Princeton Survey Research Associations May 25-June 4, 2000. Margin of error +/-3 percentage points.

supportive of using the surplus for purposes other than tax cuts. Americans appeared to desire increasing spending on domestic programs and reducing the national debt more than they are clamoring for tax cuts. When asked "how should the budget surplus be used?" nearly twice as many Americans (43%) in a 1999 Gallup Poll favored increased government spending as opposed to reducing income taxes (22%) and almost a third (30%) claimed that the surplus should be used to pay down the national debt.[25]   Increasing spending toward Social Security, Medicare, and education were all considered to be a more important priority than cutting income taxes. When asked what should be a top priority given the budget surplus, 32% said strengthening Social Security, 31% said reducing the national debt, 28% said strengthening Medicare, 25% said increasing education funding, and only 22% said cutting income taxes. At the same time, 34% said that cutting income taxes should be of low priority or no priority at all (see Table 6.5). Even as the federal government was producing record surpluses in 2000, cutting income taxes had relatively little support compared to increasing domestic and defense spending (see Figure 6.2). At the same time, Americans also consistently said that they preferred to use the surplus to reduce the national debt as opposed to cutting income taxes.

The advent of budgetary surpluses corresponded with a change in public opinion regrading the necessity of tax cuts. As Figure 6.3 displays, the American public that overwhelmingly supported tax cuts in the late 1970s became much more ambivalent about them 20 years later. In 1979, 62% of Americans agreed that "The government ought to cut taxes even if it means putting off some important things that need to be done"; twenty years later, only 21% agreed. The fact that tax cuts appeared to be a less salient issue in 1999 than it was two decades previously was an important change in public opinion. By the late 1990s, public opinion appeared to potentially present an opportunity to continue producing surpluses and reduce the national debt.

Even though public was against cutting spending on entitlements, policymakers were aided in their attempts to reduce the deficit because the public gave deficit reduction a higher priority than tax cuts. The increase of revenues due to the 1993 Budget Reconciliation Bill may have been a fluke–the revenues brought in have been much greater than anyone expected–but public opinion produced a hospitable environment for deficit reduction. Congressional inaction on the budget, therefore, was a good reflection of public opinion as the federal government produced surpluses from 1998-2001.

Figure 6.3
Change of Public Opinion on Tax Cuts

"The government ought to cut taxes even if it means putting off some important things that need to be done."

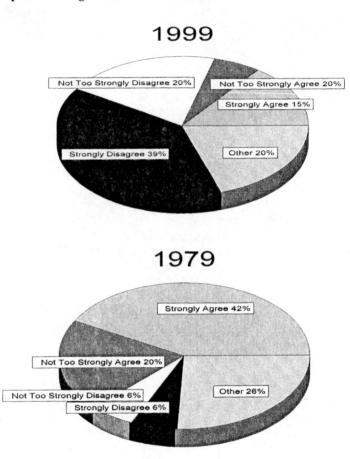

1999

Not Too Strongly Disagree 20%

Not Too Strongly Agree 20%

Strongly Agree 15%

Strongly Disagree 39%

Other 20%

1979

Strongly Agree 42%

Not Too Strongly Agree 20%

Not Too Strongly Disagree 6%

Strongly Disagree 6%

Other 26%

Source: Gallup Poll of 1,028 adults nationwide August 16-18, 1999. Margin of error +/-3 percentage points.

Conclusion

The fact that the federal government has had difficulty balancing the budget over the past three decades is due in a large part because Congress has been reacting to public opinion that has been ambivalent and inconsistent in regard to deficit reduction. The contradiction of public opinion regarding budget priorities may be inherent in a modern democracy. Representatives tend to favor budgets that run in the red because they are doing the best they can to follow the wishes of a public. As a result, there may be a representational bias in the political system which encourages deficit spending.

Endnotes

1. James Stimson, *Public Opinion in America* (Boulder, CO: Westview Press, 1991).

2. V.O. Key, *Public Opinion and American Democracy* (New York: Knopf, 1961).

3. Everett Carll Ladd, "Public Opinion and the '"Congress Problem,'" *The Public Interest* 100 (1990): 57-67.

4. Robert H. Durr, John Gilmour and Christina Wolbrecht, "Explaining Congressional Approval," *American Journal of Political Science* 41 (1997): 175-207.

5. David Kimball and Samuel Patterson, "Living Up to Expectations: Public Attitudes Toward Congress," *The Journal of Politics* 59 (1997): 701-728.

6. Kelley D. Patterson and David B. Magleby, "Public Support for Congress," *Public Opinion Quarterly* 56 (1992): 539-551.

7.Gary Jacobson, "Deficit-Cutting Politics and Congressional Elections," *Political Science Quarterly* 108 (1993): 375-402.

8. Lawrence R. Jacobs, Eric D. Lawrence, Robert Y. Shapiro, and Steven S. Smith, "Congressional Leadership on Public Opinion," *Political Science Quarterly* 113 (1998): 21-41.

9. Joseph White and Aaron Wildavsky, *The Deficit and the Public Interest* (Berkeley: University of California Press, 1989).

10. Aaron Wildavsky and Namoi Caiden, *The New Politics of the Budgetary Process*, 4th edition (New York: Longman, 2001).

11. Gallup Poll (August 8-10, 1993; Survey GO 422004, Q.19). Based on national survey of 799 interviews.

12. Ibid.

13. White and Wildavsky (1989), pp. 427-28.

14. B. Guy Peters, *The Politics of Taxation* (Cambridge, MA: Blackwell, 1991).

15. Gallup Poll (August 8-10, 1993; Survey GO 422004, Q.19). Based on national survey of 799 interviews.

16. Allen Schick, "The Majority Rules," *The Brookings Review* 14 (1996): 42-55.

17. White and Wildavsky (1989).

18. Jacobson (1993).

19. Mathew McCubbins, "Government on Lay-Away: Federal Spending and Deficits under Divided Government," *The Politics of Divided Government*, Samuel Kernell and Gary W. Cox editors (Boulder, CO: Westview Press, 1991), pp. 138-141.

20. Wildavsky and Caiden (2001).

21. Frank Newport, "Tax Cuts Have a Generic Appeal, But Are Not Voters' Highest   Priority,"   *The   Gallup   Organization* (http://www.gallup.com/releases/pr990626.asp) June 27, 1999.

22. Carolyn Webber and Aaron Wildavsky, *A History of Taxation and Expenditure in the Western World* (New York: Simon and Schuster, 1986), p. 528.

23. Allen Schick, "A Surplus, If We Can Keep It," *The Brookings Review* 18 (2000): 36-39.

24. Ibid.

25. Gallup Poll of 1,013 adults nationwide August 17-18, 1999. Margin of error +/-3 percentage points.

Chapter 7

The Parochial Nature of
Congressional Budgeting

The Paradox of Budgeting

The difficulty Congress has budgeting is in part structural and in part political. It is primarily for political reasons, however, that Congress finds it extremely difficult to produce balanced budgets. In particular, the nature of congressional representation is not conducive toward budgeting.

The difficulties Congress has in budgeting are a direct result of the nature of a representative democracy. When it comes to congressional budgeting, democratic representation is a paradox because the American public wants contradictory actions from its representatives in Congress. The public wants lower taxes, does not want its government services cut, and wants a balanced budget to boot. If the role of a member of Congress is to represent the wishes of his or her constituents, something has got to give. For the most part this has been balancing the budget.

The Nature of Congressional Representation

What does "representation" mean? There are two basic types of formalistic views of representation: 1) the authoritarian view; and 2) the accountability view. According to the authoritarian view, a representative is someone who has been authorized to act. This means that the representative has been given a right to act in behalf of a collectivity which he or she did not have before, while the represented have become responsible for the consequences of that action as if they had done it themselves.   The accountability view, in contrast, holds that a representative is someone who is to be held strictly accountable, having to answer directly to the represented for what he or she does. Representation, according to this view, means that the representative must be responsible to the represented.[1]

Whom does a representative represent?   This is called the mandate-independence controversy.   Mandate theorists hold that constituents' desires and wishes must be present in an elective representative's actions, while independence theorists hold that the representative must do what he or she thinks is right, regardless of constituent beliefs. Edmund Burke's theory of representation fits the latter view. To him, representatives should be seen as a "natural aristocracy" that represent the nation as a whole, not individual local interests. According to Burke, representatives should be viewed as and think of themselves as trustees as opposed to delegates.   Burke's concept of representation, therefore, contrasts both "descriptive representation," which holds that representation should be a mirror of the nation, and "symbolic representation," which holds that representation is just a symbol–elites make the real decisions.[2]

Politics takes form in a realm of pressures and opinions in which representatives must operate. Political representation in democratic politics requires accountability, either to the nation as a whole or to one's constituency. Unfortunately, in terms of congressional budgeting, these two objects of accountability are not always compatible.   Whereas accountability toward the nation may require spending cuts or revenue increases to balance the budget, accountability toward one's constituency may require making sure that the representative's constituency is getting their fair share of whatever spending is done. Thus, you often see the spectacle of members of Congress calling for budget cuts while simultaneously lobbying for federal funds for projects in their own district. Congress is a responsive body, but this does not necessarily make it an accountable body. Congress may be representative, but of whom?

The United States has accumulated an enormous national debt at least in part because accurate representation can lead to questionable public policy. The fiscal concerns of members of Congress are the natural outcomes of the duties of their jobs. If one duty of members of Congress is to represent the people back home, they do this well, particularly in defending existing programs. The public may want a balance between representing constituency interests and representing national interests, but they do not want this balance at any price, and their representatives act accordingly. The Burkean plea to regard the common interest above that of one's constituency is compelling, but it is often not followed. By running a deficit, the members of Congress can satisfy the demands of many particular groups (and get the political benefits of doing so) without antagonizing voters by raising taxes. Deficit spending can thereby be regarded as a reflection of the public's contrary demands, and the desire of Congress to try to accommodate them.[3]

The legislative character of the powers to tax, spend, and borrow was easily accepted by the Founding Fathers; they considered an independent "power of the purse" to be a cornerstone of a stable and effective national government. The framers of the Constitution, however, could not foresee how the congressional budget process would be transformed as the nation, and the responsibilities of government, grew. The fact that there are now 435 representatives and 100 Senators who have equal votes in their respective bodies creates problems in trying to maintain a sense of responsibility.

The emphasis of Congress on individuals, because of the nature in which our legislators are selected (elected in separate single-member constituencies in a system of weak political party cohesion), has made it difficult for Congress to balance the budget in an era where the government faces numerous demands. Furthermore, many of the problems that comprehensive budget proposals have within Congress stem from the nature of Congress as an institution and the place of Congress in the separation of powers framework of the Constitution. The organizational requirements for fiscal policy are quite different from those of representation that are characteristic of Congress. Since budgeting is not the sole mission of Congress, the criteria by which to evaluate the performance of congressional budgeting are not obvious.[4]

Congress is a thoroughly democratic institution, responsive to public opinion, attentive to constituency concerns, and highly accessible to a broad diversity of groups and interests. Its members are also very much aware of their accountability to voters. Every member's definition of the fiscal good arises in reference to concrete political and institutional circumstances. The result is an ambivalence in supporting proposals to balance the budget when faced with taxing and spending specifics. There is an almost complete disassociation between the institutional reputation of Congress and the reelection prospects of its members.

What is good for an individual member of Congress is not necessarily good for the institution as a whole. What is good for an individual congressional district, furthermore, is not necessarily good for the nation as a whole. The budget process in Congress reflects these congressional facts of life. The budget process as it is now organized tends to serve the political interests of individual members well, but not necessarily the interests of the institution as a whole. As a result, the nation too often suffers. Democracy complicates budgeting because it is widely held that spending money helps one electorally and imposing costs is politically harmful. Members of Congress can avoid making politically difficult decisions while they blame the president, the bureaucracy, or interest groups for being the real culprit for rising deficits. As Richard Fenno writes, a "legislature that cannot make tough, sensible budgetary decisions cannot govern, cannot wield its quintessential power of the purse, and cannot shape national programs and national priorities."[5]

The Macrobudget vs. Microbudget

Macroeconomic theories focus on the aggregate amounts of government spending, taxing and borrowing. Microeconomic theories, on the other hand, look more closely at individual programs, such as targeted public works jobs, or subsidies to wheat farmers.[6] Congress is designed to be a much better microbudgeter than macrobudgeter. Where the federal budget is concerned, however, macro and micro concerns often collide. For example, a representative from Iowa may favor reducing the deficit, but not through reduced farm payments. Similarly, job training programs are seen as important in urban districts, often even by those representatives who publicly call themselves fiscal conservatives. Budgeting in Congress, therefore, is not the same as budgeting in the executive branch. While it is the weaker branch dealing with the totals, Congress dominates the microbudget.

The dispersion of budget jurisdiction in Congress enables individual committees to concentrate on the parts of the budget that matter most to them. Although no committee has legislative control over the whole budget, each has a strong incentive to be vigilant regarding the matters in its jurisdiction.[7] This process is not designed for macrobudgeting. After all, in the end, a budget's totals are a sum of its parts. For legislative macrobudgeting to work, it is essential that the totals are a result of congressional decisions as opposed to the outcome of decisions beyond its control. But the current process makes it extremely difficult to plan ahead and be prepared for certain conditions that may arise.

The inability of Congress to manage the macrobudget consequences of their actions can be seen during the process of gaining support for the final version of President Clinton's budget bill in 1993. Almost every Democratic member of Congress was consulted, lobbied, and in many cases accommodated before the conference committee produced the final bill. As Congressmen John Murtha (D-PA) said, "Clinton is dealing with 258 Democrats in the House and 56 in the Senate. Every single group has something they're interested in."[8] Since the Republicans had been unanimous in their opposition from the outset, the conference committee–typically a bipartisan confrontation between the House and the Senate–was turned into a feud among Democrats. The result was numerous concessions to Democratic members who threatened to bring down the package over home-state interests.

Democratic Senators, especially, were in a good position to hold the package hostage to their demands. Dianne Feinstein, at the time a freshmen from California, was able to get a broader tax credit for research and development. Russ Feingold, another freshmen in 1993, was able to gain the inclusion of a ban of the use of growth hormones on cows into the bill. Individual House Democrats had less leverage than senators, but they also received their share of courting. Well-organized voting blocs, in particular, wielded significant influence. From the beginning, for example, the bill was certain to include tax credits for inner cities and the working poor because of the demands of the Congressional Black Caucus and its 38 House Democratic members. The end result of all this maneuvering was a bill that offered fewer spending cuts, fewer tax increases, and thus less deficit reduction. The cajoling to get members' support for the bill displays the difficulty in getting a budget through Congress intact. It is difficult to produce a budget when 535 members of Congress want to put their marks on the bill.

The tragedy of the commons describes what will happen to public consumption when no costs are imposed on the use of a common resource. The English public commons were overgrazed and destroyed until access to them was controlled through some form of price mechanism or rationing.[9] The same phenomenon applies to all use of public goods when it comes to accepting "free" benefits. In effect, we have paid our taxes, so we have a strong incentive to get as many benefits as possible. With their taxes already paid, it is in their rational self-interest to get as many benefits as possible in return. The net effect of large numbers of individuals and interest groups pushing for ever-higher benefit levels may be to produce an aggregate level of government spending that is higher than desired by any individual or group. Or conversely, ignorance of benefits received may yield a bias against taxes.[10] Unfortunately, by acting in our own interest we may produce too much of a good thing.

Members of Congress can also be viewed as constantly looking out for their own interest. As Anthony Downs postulates, members of Congress act to maximize votes. Thus, when budgeting, members ask whether or not programs are worth the cost in terms of votes gained. Congress is likely to adopt programs if more political support is to be gained than lost from that program, or vice-versa. Downs argues that public sector expenditures should be increased until the vote gain of the last dollars spent on a program was equal to the vote loss of the last dollars collected to finance that program.[11] According to this theory, deficit spending is primarily the fault of distributing benefits to get votes without looking at the macroeconomic effects of what is being done.

If both citizens and members of Congress view decisions in terms of self interest, it would be impossible for Congress to produce good macrobudgets. By focusing its energy on microbudgeting, members of Congress risk "nickel and diming" the budget to death by making sure their constituency gets their fair share. Congress is simply designed to microbudget better than macrobudget. As Congressman Ralph Regula (R-OH) stated, "Because we have a micro, micro, micro focus in Congress, we are used to dealing with programs. The big picture dissolves into a budget of smaller concerns."[12] Even though these forces have existed for many years, in a bygone era where government was smaller and budgeting less complex Congress was still able to produce balanced budgets. Beginning in the 1970s, however, the complexity of the budget began to overwhelm the traditional budgeting norms and chronic deficits began plaguing the budget process.

Senators and representatives create programs on the basis of geographic and group benefits, leaving particularism with an obvious imprint on the budget. Even though political calculations usually revolve around noneconomic components of derivative economic policy, economic components still play an important role in their decisions, especially if coalition leaders work to increase legislators' consciousness about a vote's economic and political implications. The political calculations of legislators change once they deal with explicit economic policy, where economic components are larger and more prominent than noneconomic components.[13] This is when particularism tends to dominate the congressional agenda. Electoral quests inspire both a concern for group and geographic benefits which, when pursued to excess, can produce deficits as well as a lack of concern for some of the general costs and benefits associated with governmental spending.

The Potential Problems of Parochialism

When producing the budget, members of Congress take care of state and local interests as well as promoting broad national or public interests. When it comes to budgeting, Congress is often criticized for being too caught up in local or parochial interests. Without doubt, legislators receive a good deal of pressure from their constituents on budgetary matters. As a result, members are caught between conflicting demands. Since members must appease the desires of their constituency to win reelection, national interests on the budget may often be forced to take a back seat to local interests. In fact, sometimes local and national interests are in direct conflict. The parochial nature of Congress, therefore, may be partly to blame for the nation's budgetary woes.

The potential problems of parochialism for Congress can be seen by comparing the institution to the presidency. The president, unlike Congress, is elected by the entire nation, and is expected to represent the entire nation. Though the president is undoubtedly more supportive of particular interests and groups more than others, he is also the symbolic leader for the entire nations whose success is judged by the condition of the nation as a whole. Though it is certainly legitimate to criticize the president for some of the problems in the budget process, the problems the president faces are considerably different from those of Congress. Congress is a diverse group of 535 members who representing different constituencies that have different interests and needs. Consequently, it should be expected that members of Congress will have numerous views on budgetary policy. Parochial interests make it difficult to produce a budget with the nation's collective good in mind.

One result of Congress' parochialism may be to encourage excessive spending through the process of pork barreling. A popular criticism of the congressional budget process is that in their desire to please their constituents, members of Congress try to get special projects or funds for their districts to the detriment of the budget as a whole. "Pork," however, only makes a small impact on the federal deficit.[14] Rather than encouraging excessive pork barreling, the problem of parochialism is that it forces members of Congress to look only at part of the whole budgetary puzzle. That is, parochialism may cause members to look too much at how budget proposals affect their own districts and not enough at whether the budget is in the best interests of the nation.

The Constituency and Budget Priorities

Do members of Congress tend to favor budget policies that benefit particular constituencies? It is possible that recent attempts by Congress to reduce taxes may display particular constituency biases toward the budgetary process. As a result, national interests toward other budget priorities, such as producing a balanced budget, may get less attention.

The degree to which one's constituency affects the actions of a member of Congress has extremely important implications in congressional budgeting. If a legislator is responsive to the wants of his or her constituents, it suggests that constituents have the potential of playing an important, if indirect, role in the creation of the nation's budget. At the same time, if the people are letting their budgetary demands be known, it becomes important to analyze what these demands are. It is possible that the problems in congressional budgeting are a direct result of the inconsistencies of what the public says it wants.[15]

In the tradition of American legislative politics, the legislator has the responsibility of representing his or her constituency and promoting its interests. Constituents' knowledge of their representative and his or her activities, however, is insufficient to serve as a controlling mechanism.[16] Since on numerous important policy matters members of Congress hear little from their constituents, a member of Congress has a very wide range of choices on any given issue, so far as his or her constituency is concerned.[17] Constituency interests play an important role in congressional decision-making. Since most members of Congress would like to be reelected, constituency pressures impose meaningful constraints on voting behavior.

Strong popular opinion in one's district strongly correlates to a member's vote.[18] On many budgetary issues, however, it is not clear what the preferences of one's constituents are. For most of the population below elites, there is only modest consistency among political beliefs and opinions.[19] As a result, members of Congress must rely on factors other than constituency preferences to make their voting decisions. In a landmark 1963 study, it was found that there was a high correlation between the popular opinion of a district and its representative's votes in Congress on economic issues (though the correlation was higher on civil rights than on economic issues). The instructed-delegate model of government was found to exist in Congress to a certain degree–a representative's roll call behavior was strongly influenced by the preferences of one's constituency. Ironically, the authors also concluded that members of Congress tend to overrate their visibility.[20] Most citizens do not have any idea of their representative's stands on budget issues or of attempts to get project money for the district. Only a small proportion of constituents, however, need to be aware of a representative's actions for them to become an electoral factor.

Constituency influence tends to come in two general forms. First, it comes through the member's internalization of the political orientations of the constituency in which he or she resides. Second, it comes through the member's perceptions of the needs and demands of his or her constituency.[21] Especially important to a member of Congress is the subset of voters who supported him or her in the last election. These people have the greatest potential to influence a member's legislative actions. A representative will get a greater exposure to a less heterogeneous set of constituent-voters than will be the case for the representative vis-a-vis the legally defined constituency. Members of Congress are expected to represent the subset of the constituency who voted for them.

In terms of budgeting, this means that members will work for the interests of their supporters rather than for the constituency as a whole. When budgeting, members will therefore tend to have a bias toward certain groups and certain interests. Given the nature of a members' support, it can be to the benefit of individual members of Congress to go out of their way to protect the interests of his or her electoral coalition at all costs, even if the interests of the nation, or even one's own constituency, are not properly served.

As born out by public opinion polls, people tend to dislike Congress as an institution while liking their own congressional representatives. These seemingly contradictory attitudes are the result of what Americans have come to expect of their legislative representatives. As the term denotes, voters expect legislators to "represent" them, supposedly by defending the interests of their home district, but at the same time voters expect Congress to solve the social and economic ills facing the nation as a whole. These two expectations do not necessarily go hand-in-hand; in fact, oftentimes they are in direct conflict. It is

widely held, however, that members of Congress must pay close attention
to the wants of their own constituencies if they desire to be re-elected. As
a result, members of Congress must spend a considerable amount of time
articulating their actions to the people in their districts while
simultaneously carefully monitoring the popular mood in their districts.

Table 7.1 displays Pearson correlations between district
demographics and four political variables (for an analysis of these
variables see Chapter 1). A House district's per capita income, its
percentage of people who have attended college, the percentage of its
population that is white, and the percentage of its population that lives in
rural areas are all negatively correlated with the representative's party, the
representative's ideology (as measured by the *National Journal* for the
103rd Congress), the district's vote for Clinton in 1992, and the
representative's vote on the 1993 Budget Reconciliation Bill.

This indicates that as income in a district increased, as the
number of people who attended college increased, as the number of
whites in the district increased, and as the number of people living in rural
areas increased, the district's conservatism, as measured by its vote in
presidential elections and the behavior of its representative, increased.
All of the correlations among these variables were statistically significant
with the exception of that between the representative's party and
percentage of the district that lives in rural areas. The fact that the
member's vote on the 1993 Budget Reconciliation Bill was correlated with
the per capita income, percentage white, percentage that attended college,
and percentage that lives in rural areas of a representative's district
indicates the importance of district characteristics in influencing
legislators' budgetary actions. A district's political preferences are
strongly correlated with the district's demographics.

Since senators tend to represent more demographically and
politically heterogeneous districts than do House members, the
correlations are not nearly as impressive when done for the Senate.
Because they represent entire states, senators are much more likely to face
constituencies that are less consensual in their beliefs. The relatively
small size of the Senate also makes it relatively difficult to make
generalizations about individual Senators statistically. Nevertheless, the
results shown in Table 7.1 demonstrate that there are consistent patterns
between state demographics and the political characteristics of the state
and their senators. State per capita income was positively correlated with
all of the political characteristics, and the percent with a college
education, percent white, and percent living in rural areas of a senator's

Table 7.1
Constituency Influence: Correlations between District
Demographics and Legislator Characteristics

	Per Capita Income	% College Educated	% White	% Rural
House				
Representative's Party	-0.231***	-0.236***	-0.321***	-0.082
Representatives Ideology	-0.106*	-0.136**	-0.431***	-0.246***
District Clinton Vote (1992)	-0.114*	-0.213***	-0.676***	-0.352***
Vote on 1993 Budget	-0.176***	-0.176****	-0.378***	-0.158***
Senate				
Senator's Party	0.146	-0.156	-0.157	-0.154
Senator's Ideology	0.279**	-0.075	-0.024	-0.185
State Clinton Vote (1992)	0.259**	-0.382***	-0.319***	-0.061
Vote on 1993 Budget	0.162	-0.133	-0.120	-0.103

* $p < .05$; **$p < .01$; ***$p < .001$

state were negatively correlated with all the political characteristics. These results underline the fact that members of Congress try to represent the political and budgetary views of their constituents, and these political and budgetary views can be partially determined by the demographics of a representative's district. Constituency demographics, therefore, explains some of the variation of members' budgetary actions.

Congressional budgeting is a product of the wishes of the people. As one would hope from a representative democracy, members of Congress apparently do a very good job of representing the beliefs of their constituents, at least on high visibility issues. Even if members of Congress acted solely on the basis on their own values and interests, budgeting would be difficult. Our nation's representatives, however, are expected to make budgetary decisions based on what those they represent want. As Table 4.3 shows (see Chapter 4), members of Congress tend to behave in a manner that is consistent with the prevailing beliefs of their constituents. Outside influences, such as interest groups, do affect member's decisions on the budget to some degree. But the influence of interest groups is limited by the desires of a member's constituency. The nature of representation in the United States encourages members of Congress to make decisions based on the wishes of their constituency.

Sometimes, however, congressional action may seem to contradict constituency public opinion. In such cases, it may be useful to differentiate between different part of a constituency, rather than looking at the entire constituency.

In recent years congressional Republicans proposing to reduce taxes have tended to focus on across-the-board income tax reductions that disproportionately favor the wealthy. Yet, public opinion does not seem to support this approach to tax cuts. Americans overwhelmingly believe that the wealthier are paying less than their fare share in federal taxes (see Chapter 6). Public opinion polls show that Republicans potentially faced a problem due to the fact that the public overwhelmingly felt that congressional Republicans were most interested in helping the wealthy with their proposed tax cuts. While 51 percent said that Republicans in Congress were most interested in benefitting the rich with their proposed tax cuts, only 13 percent responded that the Republicans were most interested in aiding the middle-class. This was noticeably different from the public's attitude on the Democrats proposed tax cuts. More felt that the Democrats were more interested in benefitting the middle class with their tax cut proposals (see Figure 7.1).

Why have congressional Republicans so adamantly supported tax cuts even though it seems to be contradictory to public demand? Republicans strong support of reducing taxes and the Democrats hostility to the concept may be a result of the nature of congressional representation. The Republicans are advocating a position that appeals to their political base, even though it is relatively unpopular among the populace as a whole. The differences in the tax policy orientations of the two parties, therefore, can be explained by the fact that members trying to represent their political base.

Especially important to a member of Congress is the subset of voters who supported him or her in the last election. These people have the greatest potential to influence a member's legislative actions. A representative will get a greater exposure to a less heterogeneous set of constituent-voters than will be the case for the representative vis-a-vis the legally defined constituency. Members of Congress are expected to represent the subset of the constituency who voted for them.[22] This may mean that members will work for the interests of their supporters rather

Figure 7.1
Public Opinion on Tax Proposals

"Who do you think the Republicans/Democrats in Congress are most interested in benefitting with their proposed tax cuts: the rich, the middle class, or both about equally?"

Republicans

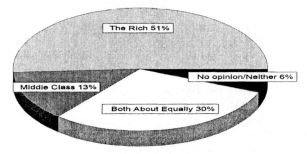

Democrats

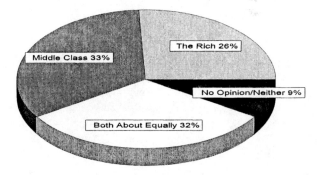

Source: Gallup Poll of 1,031 adults nationwide July 16-18, 1999. Margin of error +/-3 percentage points.

than for the constituency as a whole. Members will therefore tend to have a bias toward certain groups and certain interests. Given the nature of a members' support, it can be to the benefit of individual members of Congress to go out of their way to protect the interests and preferences of his or her electoral coalition. For Republicans, this may lead them to support tax cuts even if it is seems to contradict public opinion; for Democrats, this may lead them to support higher levels of taxation than the population as a whole favors.

Constituency interests play an important role in congressional decision-making. Since members of Congress would like to be reelected, constituency pressures impose meaningful constraints on voting behavior. Representatives will act in concurrence with the preferences of their constituents in order to get reelected.[23] Members of Congress will thus be attentive to the people that they are elected to represent. Congress, therefore, is not a neutral institution making laws which benefit all citizens of the United States equally. Since individual House districts tend to be relatively homogeneous, but heterogeneous as a whole (that is, they vary among each other), and if we expect members of Congress to be responsive to the wishes of their constituents, it follows that members of Congress will represent their constituents differently, depending upon the characteristics of their district.[24] The demographic characteristics of constituencies substantially effect the explanation of roll call votes.[25] Thus, citizen preferences may be expected to vary according to their demographic characteristics, which in turn influences the political behavior of their representatives in Congress.

Toward a Communitarian Budget?

The recent history of budgeting would look much better if it were not for the massive deficits that have accumulated over the past three decades into a staggering national debt of more than $3.5 trillion. Ending the crisis in budgeting depends on the ability to produce durable reductions in the deficit. Large deficits have brought considerable political difficulty. Congress and the president have had considerably difficulty producing balanced budgets, despite the fact that everyone said they wanted to do so, because the problem has become so overwhelming. As much as Congress wanted to reign in deficits, it has feared the solutions–such as raising taxes or Social Security cuts–even more. Budgeting has become a hostage to larger political forces which is the result of the imbalance between claims and resources. Democratic governments unquestionably are better at redistributing benefits than redistributing resources.[26]

As government has grown more complex, fights over economic policy have increased. The budget process has to meet many conflicting pressures. With higher expectations for public services, the indexing of a number of benefits, and relatively sluggish economic performance over the past three decades or so, Congress has been unable to cope with the new economics of the budgetary process.

Limiting congressional activism is the fact that all of the varying elements in the American political creed unite in imposing limits on power and on the institutions of government. Americans have an antipower ethic. Compared to other peoples, Americans have relatively high trust in each other, but a much lower trust in government.[27] At the same time, because we are taught to believe in the necessity of constitutional checks and balances, we place little faith in societal checks and balances.[28] This creates an environment in which Congress is not only constrained to make the politically difficult budgetary decisions it needs to make by the antigovernment ethic of the American people, but it is also constrained by the constitutional checks on the body as well. Congress, however, needs to be able to react to a rapidly changing budgetary environment. By continuing to constrain Congress with constitutional and antipower societal checks, Congress risks not being able to meet the budgeting needs of the 21st century. The country's massive deficit is coming at a particularly inappropriate time in American economic history. The relatively small labor force of the first half of the next century will have to be substantially more productive to achieve a rising standard of living for itself and for the relatively large retired population simultaneously.[29]

Rather than viewing Congress as the enemy, it would be more constructive for the American public to acknowledge the difficult decisions Congress is forced to make in an era of shrinking resources. Such a desire can be seen in the communitarian approach to the problem of the massive accumulation of national debt, which holds "that our political community represents a covenant between ourselves, past generations of Americans, and Americans yet to be born. We have no right to squander our inheritance; we do have a responsibility to pass on to posterity a nation at least as united, prosperous, and filled with opportunity as the one we received. A legacy of declining living standards and shrinking opportunities represents moral, not just economic, failure. To the extent that deficits and debt contribute to this outcome, their reduction is not an option but rather a duty."[30] The communitarian budget philosophy is that the highest obligation of citizenship is to challenge leaders to appeal to a much larger obligation: serving the broad public interest.[31]

The communitarian approach to budgeting rests on the belief in the possibility of public moral dialogue and in the capacity of citizens to respond to it. Advocates of communitarian budgeting believe that democratic citizens must be moved by shared principles rather than by particular interests. The responsibility of democratic political leadership, according to this view, is to unite the citizenry by appealing to the better side of our nature. Our nation's economic policies should promote our shared purposes and reflect our shared values.[32] The principle of fairness should determine who must sacrifice the most when it comes to measures to reduce the deficit. Entitlement reform, for example, should be reformed to ensure that wealthy people receive no more than their fair share of these taxpayer-financed benefits. As it stands today, federal entitlement spending, including retirement and health programs, favors people with incomes above $100,000.[33]

The communitarian ideal for budgeting may be idealistic, but it should be considered a plausible alternative to our current conflictual budget process. The traditional American focus is on the individual. Budgeting, however, by its very nature, requires us to think of the well-being of society as a whole.

Structurally, Congress, as well as the American political system in general, is not designed in a manner conducive toward budgeting. Though many of the seemingly problematic features of the congressional budget process were not designed by the Founding Fathers, the manner in which the political institutions of the United States were designed may be partly to blame for the difficulty Congress has in budgeting. In their desire to limit the "tyranny of the majority," the Founding Fathers created a legislative body that was destined to be inefficient. Yet, while Congress is not structured in a manner that makes it easy to pass the complex legislation that the budget has become in the 21st century, the structure of Congress does not make it impossible to enact a sensible budget either.

Budgeting for a country of more than 280 million people, however, requires the nation's representatives to compromise relatively narrow interests for the well being of the entire nation. It has been found that the politicians elected to Congress tend to believe that the well-being of the nation as a whole is the most important goal for a public servant.[34] Yet the actions of members of Congress are not always consistent with this ideal. The budget process requires a Congress that is able to make macro-level decisions, something Congress has, to a significant degree, been unable to do when it comes to budgeting.

Conclusion

When making decisions on the budget, members of Congress are influenced considerably by their constituents. The nation's representatives and senators must continuously make difficult budgetary decisions on matters which the constituents they represent have little understanding or knowledge. Yet, the nature of representation in this country, in which the nation's legislators are elected from individual districts representing distinct constituencies, encourages parochial behavior by our legislators. That is, members of Congress are limited in the range of what they can do with the budget because of the restraints of constituency representation. Budgeting requires the nation's diverse interests to compromise. But each individual constituency, which may have strong budget preferences of its own, demands that its representative be attentive to its needs. The nature of representation in the United States is not conducive toward producing the nation's budget.

Congress tends to be a representative body; therefore, problems exist when the public cannot make up its mind or sends contradictory signals to their representatives. Government has a hard time moving to rectify even obvious problems–and this is a traditional problem in American history. Almost all members of Congress want to make good public policy but they also want to win reelection. Given that reelection is probably the primary goal for most, good public policy will take the back seat to electoral goals. Furthermore, people generally do not want brave and bold representatives, as their actions at the ballot box usually indicate. Budgeting, however, requires brave and bold representatives.

Since the United States is a representative democracy, such changes in how Congress budgets will only happen if the American public approves. Even as the federal government produces massive annual deficits, however, the political impediments to improving the budget process are immense. Members of Congress are trapped between a desire to reduce the deficit and to do what their constituents expect them to do by protecting them from losing their benefits and from paying higher taxes. Our representatives in Congress follow popular opinion extremely closely–maybe too closely when it comes to budgeting. At the same time, the public is extremely critical of Congress as an institution for maintaining such large deficits–public opinion of Congress has never been lower. The paradox for members of Congress, therefore, is that the people that they represent are sending them conflicting messages as to what their budgeting priorities should be. Unless these contradictory desires are modified, the nature of Congress as a representative body makes congressional budgeting destined to be viewed as flawed and inadequate.

Congressional budgeting is a product of the wishes of the people. As one would hope from a representative democracy, members of Congress apparently do a very good job of representing the beliefs of their constituents, at least on high visibility issues. But what if the beliefs of constituents are vague and inconsistent? This can become a major obstacle for members of Congress when they are trying to produce a budget.

Even if members of Congress acted solely on the basis on their own values and interests, budgeting would be difficult. Our nation's representatives, however, are expected to make budgetary decisions based on what those they represent want. Members of Congress tend to behave in a ideological manner that is remarkably consistent with the prevailing beliefs of their constituents. Outside influences, such as interest groups and the media, do affect member's decisions on the budget to some degree. But the influence of interest groups is limited by the desires of a member's constituency. The nature of representation in the United States encourages members of Congress to make decisions based on the wishes of their constituency.

The United States is a vast and diverse nation. Since the nation's elected representatives strongly reflect the beliefs and values of their constituents, Congress itself is a diverse group, if not demographically then in the terms of the beliefs its members bring to the body. In terms of congressional budget this is problematic. Nothing is more political than public budgeting, as opposing sides attempt to gain their fair share of the budgetary pie. In a country with such varied views about what the national budget should look like, compromise is a necessity.

Compromise, however, is difficult. Members of Congress are torn between a desire to make good public policy on the one hand, which requires compromising with other members of the legislative and executive branches, and a desire to win reelection, which may encourage legislators to take politically unrealistic budgetary stands in order to appease one's primary supporters back home. Despite the prevailing belief that members of Congress are out of touch with the beliefs of ordinary people, members of Congress follow public opinion closely. This may be part of the problem, in terms of budgeting, because the public is largely unaware of budgetary specifics. Following the wishes of the people may be desirable for a democratic nation in general. But the wishes of the people may be a poor guide when it comes to budgeting.

Endnotes

1. Hanna Pitkin, *The Concept of Representation* (Berkeley: University of California Press, 1967).

2. Ibid.

3. Patrick Fisher, "Political Explanations for the Difficulties in Congressional Budgeting," *Social Science Journal* 36 (1999): 149-161.

4. Mark Kamlet and David Mowery, "The First Decade of the Congressional Budget Act: Legislative Imitation and Adaptation in Budgeting." *Government Budgeting*, Albert Hyde ed. (Pacific Grove, CA: Brooks Cole Publishing Company, 1992), p. 128.

5. Richard F. Fenno, *The Emergence of a Senate Leader: Pete Domenici and the Reagan Budget* (Washington, D.C.: CQ Press, 1991), p. 42.

6. John Cranford, *Budgeting for America* , 2nd ed. (Washington, D.C.: CQ Press, 1989), p. 23.

7. John Cogan, Timothy Murris, and Allen Schick, *The Budget Puzzle* (Stanford, CA: Stanford University Press, 1994), p. 105.

8. Janet Hook, "Conference Without Walls," *Congressional Quarterly* (August 7, 1993), p. 2128.

9. Garrett James Hardin, *Population, Evolution and Birth Control: A Collage of Controversial Ideas, Assembled by Garret Hardin*, 2nd ed. (San Francisco: W.H. Freeman, 1969).

10. Anthony Downs, "Why the Government Budget is Too Small in a Democracy," *World Politics* 12 (1960): 541-563.

11. Anthony Downs, *An Economic Theory of Democracy* (New York: Harper and Row, 1957).

12. Ibid., p. 9.

13. R. Douglas Arnold, *The Logic of Congressional Action* (New Haven: Yale University Press), p. 153.

14. Aaron Wildavsky and Naomi Caiden, *The New Politics of the Budgetary Process*, 4th ed. (New York: Longman, 2001).

15. Patrick Fisher, "Congressional Budgeting Priorities: A Representational Perspective," *Political Chronicle* 14 (2002): 33-47.

16. Aage Clausen, *How Congressmen Decide: A Policy Focus* (New York: St. Martin's Press, 1973), p. 19.

17. Lewis Anthony Dexter, *The Sociology and Politics of Congress* (Chicago: Rand McNally, 1969), chapter 8.

18. John Kingdon, *Congressmen's Voting Decisions*, 3rd ed. (Ann Arbor: University of Michigan Press, 1989).

19. Murray Edelman, *Politics as Symbolic Action* (Chicago: Markham Publishing, 1971), p. 5.

20. Warren E. Miller and Donald E Stokes, "Constituency Influence in Congress," *American Political Science Review* 57 (1963): 45-56.

21. Clausen (1973).

22. Richard Fenno, *Homestyle* (Boston: Little, Brown and Company, 1978).

23. Anthony Downs (1957).

24. Louis A. Froman, *Congressmen and their Constituencies* (Chicago: Rand McNally, 1963).

25. Benjamin I. Page, Robert Y. Shapiro, Paul Gronke and Robert W. Rosenberg, "Constituency, Party, and Representation in Congress," *Public Opinion Quarterly* 48 (1984): 741-756.

26. Allen Schick, *The Capacity to Budget* (Washington: The Urban Institute, 1990), p. 223.

27. Samuel Huntington, *American Politics: The Promise of Disharmony* (Cambridge, MA: Belknap Press, 1981), chapter 3.

28. Robert Dahl, *Preface to Democratic Theory* (Chicago: University of Chicago Press, 1956), p. 83.

29. Alice Rivlin, "The Continuing Search for a Popular Tax," *AEA Papers and Proceedings* 79 (1989): 113-117.

30. William Galston, "A Communitarian Budget: Deficit Reduction and Job Creation," *The Responsive Community* 3 (1992): 7-9.

31. Donald F. Kettl, *Deficit Politics* (New York: Longman, 2003), p. 176.

32. Ibid., p. 7.

33. Robert Shapiro, "A New Covenant for Reforming Entitlements," *The Responsive Community* 3 (1992): 10-14.

34. William Keefe and Morris Ogul, *The American Legislative Process* (Englewood Cliffs, NJ: Prentice-Hall, 1993), p. 73.

Bibliography

Adler, E. Scott. 2000. "Constituency Characteristics and the 'Guardian' Model of Appropriations Subcommittees 1959-1998." *American Journal of Political Science* 44: 104-114.

Anderson, Gary. 1987. "The U.S. Federal Deficit and National Debt: A Political and Economic History." *Deficits*, James Buchanan, Charles Rowley and Robert Tollison eds., pp. 9-35. New York: Basil Blackwell Ltd.

Anderson, Lee, Meredith Watts, and Allen Wilcox. 1966. *Legislative Roll-Call Analysis*. Evanston: Northwestern University Press.

Arnold, R. Douglas. 1990. *The Logic of Congressional Action*. New Haven: Yale University Press.

Bailey, Michael and David W. Brady. 1998. "Heterogeneity and Representation: The Senate and Free Trade." *American Journal of Political Science* 42: 524-544.

Barro, R.J. 1974. "Are Government Bonds Net Wealth?" *Journal of Political Economy* 82: 1095-1117.

Berry, William and David Lowery. 1987. "Explaining the Size of the Public Sector." *Journal of Politics* 49: 401-440.

Birnbaum, Jefferey and Alan Murray. 1987. *Showdown at Gucci Gulch*. New York: Random House.

Brady, David. 1973. *Congressional Voting in a Partisan Era*. Lawrence: University of Kansas Press.

Brembeck, Cole S. 1991. *Congress, Human Nature, and the Federal Debt*. New York: Praeger.

Buchanan, James. 1977. "Why Does Government Grow?" *Budgets and*

Bureaucrats: The Sources of Government Growth, Thomas Borcherding ed., pp. 3-18. Durham: Duke University Press.

Caiden, Naomi. 1983. "The Politics of Subtraction." *Making Economic Policy in Congress*, Allen Schick ed., pp. 100-130. Washington: AEI.

Clausen, Aage. 1973. *How Congressmen Decide: A Policy Focus*. New York: St. Martin's Press.

Cogan, John, Timothy Muris and Allen Schick. 1994. *The Budget Puzzle*. Stanford: Stanford University Press.

Cohen, Jeffrey, Michael Krassa and John Hamman. 1991. "The Impact of Presidential Campaigning on Midterm U.S. Elections." *American Political Science Review* 85: 165-178.

Converse, Philip. 1964. "The Stability of Belief Elements Over Time." *Ideology and Discontent*, David Apter, ed. New York: Free Press.

Crain, W. Mark. 1987. "Legislatures and the Durability of Deficits." *Deficits*, James Buchanan, Charles Rowley, and Robert Tollison eds., pp. 281-288. New York: Basil Blackwell Ltd.

Cranford, John. 1989. *Budgeting for America*, 2nd edition. Washington: CQ Press.

Dahl, Robert. 1956. *A Preface to Democratic Theory*. Chicago: University of Chicago Press.

Dexter, Lewis Anthony. 1969. *The Sociology and Politics of Congress*. Chicago: Rand McNally.

Dionne, E.J. 2000. "Why Americans Hate Politics: A Reprise." *The Brookings Review* 18: 8-11.

Downs, Anthony. 1957. *An Economic Theory of Democracy*. New York: Harper and Row.

_____. 1960. "Why the Government Budget Is Too Small in a Democracy." *World Politics* 12: 541-563.

Durr, Robert H., John Gilmour and Christina Wolbrecht. 1997. "Explaining Congressional Approval." *American Journal of Political Science* 41: 175-207.

Edelman, Murray. 1971. *Politics as Symbolic Action*. Chicago: Markham Publishing Company.

Edwards, George. 1980. *Presidential Influence in Congress*. San Francisco: W.H. Freeman and Company.

Ellwood, John W. 1984. "Budget Reforms and Interchamber Relations." *Congressional Budgeting*. W. Thomas Wander, F. Ted Herbert and Gary Copeland eds., pp. 100-132. Baltimore: John Hopkins

University Press.

Fenno, Richard F. 1966. *The Power of the Purse*. Boston: Little, Brown and Company.

_____. 1973. *Congressmen in Committees*. Boston: Little, Brown and Company.

_____. 1978. *Home Style*. Boston: Little, Brown and Company.

_____. 1991. *The Emergence of a Senate Leader: Pete Domenici and the Reagan Budget*. Washington: CQ Press.

Fiorina, Morris. 1974. *Representatives, Roll Calls, and Constituents*. Lexington, MA: Lexington.

_____. 1996. *Divided Government*, 2nd edition. Boston: Allyn and Bacon.

Fisher, Louis. 1985. "Ten Years After the Budget Act: Still Searching for Controls." *Public Budgeting* 5: 3-28.

Fisher, Patrick. 1997. "Committees and the Budget Process: How Representative are Congressional Budgeting Committees?" *Southeastern Political Review* 25: 769-780.

_____. 1999. "Political Explanations for the Difficulties in Congressional Budgeting." *The Social Science Journal* 36: 149-161.

_____. 1999. "The Prominence of Partisanship in the Congressional Budget Process." *Party Politics* 5: 225-236.

_____. 2002. "The Success of the 1993 Budget Reconciliation Bill at Reducing the Federal Budget Deficit." *The Review of Policy Research* 19: 30-43.

_____. 2002. "Congressional Budget Priorities: A Representational Perspective." *Political Chronicle* 14: 33-47.

_____. 2003. "In the Black: Explanations for the Federal Budget Surplus." *Social Science Journal* 40: 49-63.

Franklin, Daniel P. 1993. *Making Ends Meet*. Washington: CQ Press.

Galston, William. 1992. "A Communitarian Budget: Deficit Reduction and Job Creation." *The Responsive Community* 3: 7-9.

Gilmour, John B. 1990. *Reconcilable Differences?* Berkeley: University of California Press.

Haas, Lawarence. 1990. *Running on Empty*. Homewood, IL: Business One Irwin.

Hall, Richard and Bernard Grofman. 1990. "The Committee Assignment Process and the Conditional Nature of Committee Bias." *American Political Science Review* 84: 1149-1166.

Hansen, Susan. 1983. "Extraction: The Politics of State Taxation."

Politics in the American States, Virginia Gray, Herbert Jacob, and Kenneth Vines, eds., pp. 335-358. Glenveiw, IL: Scott, Foresman and Company.

Hardin, Garett James. 1969. *Population, Evolution and Birth Control; A Collage of Controversial Ideas, Assembled by Garrett Hardin,* 2nd edition. San Francisco: W.H. Freeman.

Hartz, Louis. 1955. *The Liberal Tradition in America.* New York: Harcourt, Brace and World.

Huntington, Samuel. 1981. *American Politics: The Promise of Disharmony.* Cambridge. MA: Belknap Press.

Ippolito, Dennis S. 1981. *Congressional Spending.* Ithaca: Cornell University Press.

_____. 2003. *Why Budgets Matter: Budget Policy and American Politics.* University Park: Pennsylvania State University Press.

Jacobs, Lawrence R., Eric D. Lawrence, Robert Y. Shapiro, and Steven S. Smith. 1998. "Congressional Leadership on Public Opinion." *Political Science Quarterly* 113: 21-41.

Jacobson, Gary. 1993. "Deficit-Cutting Politics and Congressional Elections." *Political Science Quarterly* 108: 375-402.

Jones, Bryan D., Tracy Sulkin, and Heather A. Larsen. 2003. "Policy Punctuations in American Political Institutions." *American Political Science Review* 97: 151-169.

Kamlet, Mark and David Mowery. 1992. "The First Decade of the Congressional Budget Act: Legislative Imitation and Adaptation in Budgeting." *Government Budgeting,* Albert Hyde ed., pp. 119-134. Pacific Grove, CA: Brooks Cole Publishing Company.

Keefe, William and Morris Ogul. 1993. *The American Legislative Process.* Englewood Cliffs, NJ: Prentice-Hall.

Kettl, Donald F. 2003. *Deficit Politics.* New York: Longman.

Key, V.O. 1940. "The Lack of Budgetary Theory." *American Political Science Review* 34: 1137-1140.

Keynes, John Maynard. 1937. *The General Theory of Employment, Interest, and Money.* New York: Harcourt Brace Jovanovich.

Killian, Linda. 1998. *The Freshmen.* Boulder: Westview Press.

Kimball, David and Samuel Patterson. 1997. "Living Up to Expectations: Public Attitudes Toward Congress." *The Journal of Politics* 59: 701-728

Kingdon, John. 1989. *Congressmen's Voting Decisions,* 3rd edition. Ann Arbor: University of Michigan Press.

Koven, Steven. 1988. *Ideological Budgeting.* New York: Praeger.

Krehbiel, Keith. 1990. "Are Congressional Committees Composed of Preference Outliers?" *American Political Science Review* 84: 149-164.

Ladd, Everett Carll. 1990. "Public Opinion and the 'Congress Problem.'" *The Public Interest* 100: 57-67.

Larson, Stephanie Greco. 1990. "Information and Learning in a Congressional District: A Social Experiment." *American Journal of Political Science* 34: 1102-1118.

Lee, Robert and Ronald Johnson. 1994. *Public Budgeting Systems*, 5th edition. Gaithersburg, MD: Aspen Publishers.

Leloup, Lance. 1977. *Budgetary Politics*. Brunswick, OH: King's Court Press.

_____. 1980. *The Fiscal Congress*. Westport, CT: Greenwood Press.

_____. 1989. "Fiscal Policy and Congressional Politics." *Congressional Politics*, Christopher J. Deering ed., pp. 262-283. Pacific Grove, CA: Brooks/Cole.

Lewis, Verne. 1952. "Toward a Theory of Budgeting." *Public Administration Review* 12: 43-54.

Lindbloom, Charles. 1959. "The Science of Muddling Through." *Public Administration Review* 39: 517-26.

Lowery, David and William Berry. 1983. "The Growth of Government in the United States." *American Journal of Political Science* 27: 665-94.

McCubbins, Mathew. 1991. "Government on Lay-Away: Federal Spending and Deficits under Divided Government." *The Politics of Divided Government*, Samuel Kernell and Gary W. Cox eds., pp. 138-141. Boulder: Westview Press.

Meyers, Ron T. 1994. *Strategic Budgeting*. Ann Arbor: University of Michigan Press.

Mezey, Michael. 1989. *Congress, the President, and Public Policy*. Boulder: Westview Press.

Miller, Warren and Donald Stokes. 1963. "Constituency Influence in Congress." *Elections and the Political Order*, Angus Campbell, Phillip Converse, Warren Miller, and Donald Stokes eds., pp. 351-372. New York: John Wiley and Sons.

Morgan, Ivan W. 1995. *Deficit Government*. Chicago: Ivan R. Dee.

Ogilvie, Donald. 1981. "Constitutional Limits and the Federal Budget." *The Congressional Budget Process after Five Years*, Rudolph Penner, ed., pp. 101-134. Wahington: AEI.

Page, Benjamin I., Robert Y. Shapiro, Paul Gronke and Robert W.

Rosenberg. 1984. "Constituency, Party, and Representation in Congress." *Public Opinion Quarterly* 48: 741-756.

Pascall, Glenn. 1985. *The Trillion Dollar Budget*. Seattle: University of Washington Press.

Patterson, Kelley D. and David B. Magelby. 1992. "Public Support for Congress." *Public Opinion Quarterly* 56: 539-551.

Penner, Rudolph G. and Alan J. Abramson. 1988. *Broken Purse Strings: Congressional Budgeting, 1974-1988*. Washington: The Urban Institute Press.

Peters, B. Guy. 1991. *The Politics of Taxation*. Cambridge, MA: Blackwell.

Pitkin, Hanna. 1967. *The Concept of Representation*. Berkeley: University of California Press.

Pitsvada, Bernard. 1988. "The Executive Budget–An Idea Whose Time Has Passed." *Public Budgeting and Finance*, Spring 1988: 85-94.

Poole, Keith T. and Howard Rosenthal. 1997. *A Political-Economic History of Roll Call Voting*. New York: Oxford University Press.

Rhode, David. 1992. "Electoral Forces, Political Agendas, and Partisanship in the House and the Senate." *The Postreform Congress*, Rodger Davidson ed., pp. 27-47. New York: St. Martin's Press.

Rivers, Douglas and Nancy Rose. 1985. "Passing the President's Program." *American Journal of Political Science* 29: 183-196.

Rivlin, Alice. 1987. "Why and How to Cut the Deficit." *A Nation in Debt*, Richard Fink and Jack High eds., pp. 258-265. Frederick, MD: University Press.

_____. 1989. "The Continuing Search for a Popular Tax." *AEA Papers and Proceedings* 79: 113-117.

Rose, Melody. 2001. "Divided Government and the Rise of Social Regulation." *Policy Studies Journal* 29: 611-626.

Rose, Richard. 1986. "Maximizing Tax Revenue While Minimizing Political Costs." *Journal of Public Policy* 5: 289-320.

Rubin, Irene. 2003. *Balancing the Federal Budget*. New York: Chatham House.

Sabato, Larry. 1988. *The Party's Just Begun*. Glenview, IL: Scott, Forseman and Company.

Schattsneider, E.E. 1960. *The Semisovereign People*. New York: Holt, Rinehart and Winston.

Schick, Allen. 1980. *Congress and Money*. Washington: AEI.
_____. 1990. *The Capacity to Budget*. Washington: The Urban Institute.
_____. 1996. "The Majority Rules." *The Brookings Review* 14: 42-55.
_____. 2000. "A Surplus, If We Can Keep It." *The Brookings Review* 18: 36-39.
Schier, Steven. 1992. *A Decade of Deficits*. Albany: SUNY Press.
Serra, George and David Moon. 1994. "Casework, Issue Positions, and Voting in Congressional Elections: A District Analysis." *The Journal of Politics* 56: 200-213.
Shannon, W. Wayne. 1968. *Party, Constituency and Congressional Voting*. Baton Rouge: LSU Press.
Shapiro, Robert. 1992. "A New Covenant for Reforming Entitlements." *The Responsive Community* 3: 10-14.
Shuman, Howard E. 1988. *Politics and the Budget*, 2nd ed. Englewood Cliffs, NJ: Prentice Hall.
Sinclair, Barbara. 1993. "House Majority Party Leadership in an Era of Divided Control." *Congress Reconsidered*, 5th edition., Lawrence Dodd and Bruce Oppenheimer eds., pp. 237-258. Washington: CQ Press.
Smith, Adam. 1961. *An Inquiry into the Nature and Causes of the Wealth of Nations*. New Rochelle, NY: Arlington House.
Smith, Eric. 1989. *The Unchanging American Voter*. Berkeley: University of California Press.
Smith, Steven. 1993. "Forces of Change in Senate Party Leadership and Organization." *Congress Reconsidered*, 5th edition, Lawrence Dodd and Bruce Oppenheimer eds., pp. 259-290. Washington: CQ Press.
Smith, Steven and Christopher Deering. 1990. *Committees in Congress*. Washington: CQ Press.
Sorauf, Frank and Paul Allen Beck. 1988. *Party Politics in America*, 6th edition. Glenview, IL: Scott, Foresman and Company.
Steinmo, Sven. 1993. *Taxation and Democracy*. New Haven: Yale University Press.
Stimson, James. 1991. *Public Opinion in America*. Boulder: Westview Press.
Stonecash, Jeffrey. 2000. *Class and Party in American Politics*. Boulder: Westview Press.
Strahan, Randall. 1993. "Dan Rostenkowski: A Study in Congressional Power." *Congress Reconsidered*, 5th edition. Lawrence Dodd

Lawrence Dodd and Bruce Oppenheimer eds., pp. 189-210. Washington: CQ Press.

Su, Tsai-Tsu, Mark Kamlet, and David Mowery. 1993. "Modeling U.S. Budgetary and Fiscal Policy Outcomes: A Disaggregated, Systemwide Perspecitve." *American Journal of Political Science* 37: 213-245.

Taylor, Andrew. 2002. "The Ideological Roots of Deficit Reduction Policy." *The Review of Policy Research* 19: 11-29.

Webber, Carolyn and Aaron Wildavsky. 1986. *A History of Taxation and Expenditure in the Western World.* New York: Simon and Schuster.

White, Joseph and Aaron Wildavsky. 1989. *The Deficit and the Public Interest.* Berkeley: University of California Press.

Wildavsky, Aaron and Naomi Caiden. 2001. *The New Politics of the Budgetary Process*, 4th edition. New York: Longman.

Index